The West
and the World
since 1945

Fourth Edition

The West and the World since 1945

Fourth Edition

Glenn Blackburn
Clinch Valley College of the University of Virginia

St. Martin's Press   New York

To my wife, Jere

Manager, publishing services: Emily Berleth
Packaging project editor: Kalea Chapman
Project management: Richard Steins
Photo research: Inge King
Cover design: Donna Lee Dennison
Cover map: Courtesy of Bruce Jones Design

Library of Congress Catalog Card Number: 94-80111

Manufactured in the United States of America.

0 9 8 7 6
f e d c b a

For information, write:
St. Martin's Press, Inc.
175 Fifth Avenue
New York, NY 10010

ISBN: 0-312-11193-2

Contents

Preface

What should an intelligent citizen know about the world today? That is the question the fourth edition of *The West and the World since 1945* seeks to address. The book analyzes the most fundamental developments of contemporary history in terms of four themes:

1. The conflict between the United States and the Soviet Union after World War II and the recent collapse of Communist regimes in the former Soviet Union and in the Eastern European nations
2. The economic prosperity in Western Europe, North America, and Japan
3. The struggle of many nations in Asia, Africa, and Latin America to achieve political and economic independence and some degree of economic prosperity
4. The ideas and beliefs that will largely determine how Western people react to and deal with the issues and problems of a nuclear age

Too often, those who study contemporary history are overwhelmed by the sheer mass of information available and by the complexity of events in the contemporary world. By adopting a thematic approach, I have tried to find some order in the chaos and to make the study of contemporary history more intelligible.

The West and the World since 1945 was designed to be used in a variety of ways. It can serve as a supplemental text in Western Civilization or World Civilization survey courses. It can be used as a core text for undergraduate courses in contemporary history, in which case the bibliographical essays at the end of the chapters suggest sources for additional reading. Or it can be used as a reference text for courses in contemporary economics, political science, and sociology.

I would like to express my appreciation to all those who assisted me in preparing this book. They include Major Daniel Bryant, United States Air Force Academy; Andrew F. Clark, University of North Carolina at Wilmington; Robin F. Fabel, Auburn University; Ted Kluz, Auburn University at Montgomery; Patrick O'Neil, Broome Community College; Eugene Rasor, Emory and Henry College; Douglas Richmond, University of Texas at Arlington; Robert Welborn, Clayton State College; George Munro, Virginia Commonwealth University; the staff of the Clinch Valley College library; and the staff of St. Martin's Press, especially Louise Waller and Lynnette Blevins.

Finally, and most important, I should add that I would never have finished this book without the constant support and encouragement of my wife, Jere.

Glenn Blackburn

The West
and the World
since 1945

Fourth Edition

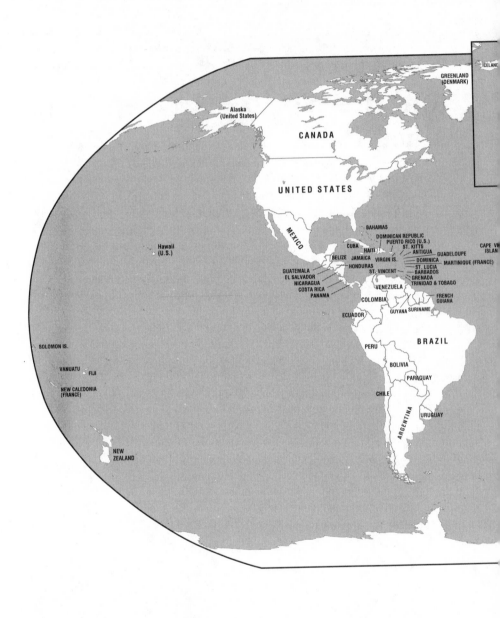

ICELAND

GREENLAND
(DENMARK)

Alaska
(United States)

CANADA

UNITED STATES

Hawaii
(U.S.)

BAHAMAS

DOMINICAN REPUBLIC
PUERTO RICO (U.S.)
CUBA   ST. KITTS
HAITI   ANTIGUA
                    GUADELOUPE   CAPE V
BELIZE   JAMAICA VIRGIN IS. DOMINICA   ISLAN
                            ST. LUCIA MARTINIQUE (FRANCE)
GUATEMALA HONDURAS ST. VINCENT BARBADOS
EL SALVADOR   GRENADA
NICARAGUA   VENEZUELA TRINIDAD & TOBAGO
COSTA RICA
PANAMA   COLOMBIA   FRENCH
                                GUIANA
            ECUADOR   GUYANA SURINAME

SOLOMON IS.   PERU   BRAZIL

VANUATU   FIJI   BOLIVIA

NEW CALEDONIA   PARAGUAY
(FRANCE)
                        CHILE
                                ARGENTINA URUGUAY

NEW
ZEALAND

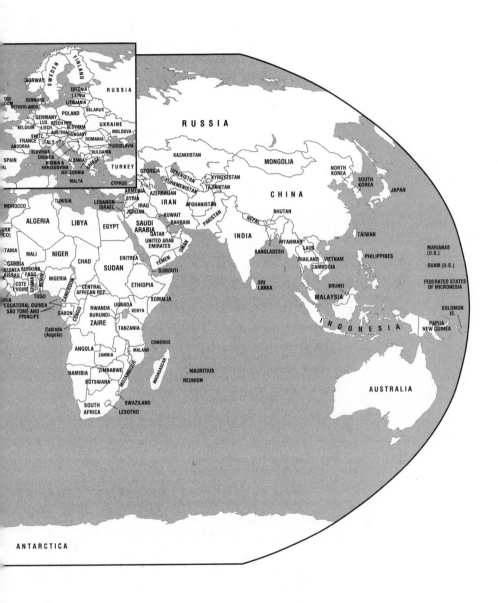

NORWAY
SWEDEN
FINLAND
RUSSIA
ESTONIA
LATVIA
LITHUANIA
TED
DENMARK
NETHERLANDS
DOM
BELARUS
GERMANY
POLAND
LUX.
CZECH REP.
BELGIUM
LIECH.
SLOVAKIA
SWITZ.
AUSTRIA
HUNGARY
UKRAINE
MOLDOVA
FRANCE
ANDORRA
SLOVENIA
ROMANIA
CROATIA
BOSNIA &
ALBANIA
YUGOSLAVIA
HERZEGOVINA
BULGARIA
MACEDONIA
ITALY
GREECE
TURKEY
MALTA
CYPRUS

AL

RUSSIA

KAZAKHSTAN

MONGOLIA

NORTH
KOREA

SOUTH
KOREA

JAPAN

GEORGIA
UZBEKISTAN
KYRGYZSTAN
ARMENIA
TURKMENISTAN
TAJIKISTAN
AZERBAIJAN
SYRIA
IRAN
LEBANON
ISRAEL
IRAQ
AFGHANISTAN
JORDAN
KUWAIT
MOROCCO
TUNISIA
SAUDI
BAHRAIN
PAKISTAN
ARABIA
QATAR
ALGERIA
LIBYA
EGYPT
UNITED ARAB
EMIRATES

CHINA

NEPAL
BHUTAN

INDIA

TAIWAN

CO)

TANIA
MALI
NIGER
CHAD

OMAN

MYANMAR
BANGLADESH
LAOS

MARIANAS
(U.S.)

GAMBIA
GUINEA
BURKINA
BISSAU
FASO
SUDAN
ERITREA
YEMEN

THAILAND
VIETNAM
CAMBODIA

PHILIPPINES

GUAM (U.S.)

COTE
D'IVOIRE
NIGERIA
DJIBOUTI

FEDERATED STATES
OF MICRONESIA

RIA
CENTRAL
AFRICAN REP.
ETHIOPIA

SRI
LANKA

BRUNEI

EQUATORIAL GUINEA
SÃO TOMÉ AND
PRINCIPE
GABON
CONGO
UGANDA
SOMALIA
RWANDA
BURUNDI
KENYA

MALAYSIA

SOLOMON
IS.

ZAIRE

INDONESIA

PAPUA
NEW GUINEA

Cabinda
(Angola)
TANZANIA

COMOROS

ANGOLA
ZAMBIA
MALAWI

MAURITIUS
REUNION

NAMIBIA
ZIMBABWE
BOTSWANA

MADAGASCAR

MOZAMBIQUE

AUSTRALIA

SOUTH
AFRICA
SWAZILAND
LESOTHO

ANTARCTICA

Introduction

The study of contemporary history is both exhilarating and frightening. It is exhilarating because the contemporary period is characterized by so many positive developments: a greatly improved standard of living for many people; better health care and a longer life span for most; and greater freedom and economic opportunity, at least for people who live in Europe and North America. It is frightening because the contemporary period includes so much that is terrible: the threat of nuclear destruction; environmental despoliation; the poverty of many countries existing amidst the affluence of the industrialized nations.

For any student of contemporary history, the challenge is to find a way of understanding the complexity and variety of our time. In this book, we look at contemporary history—the period from 1945 to the present—in terms of four themes: the Cold War between the United States and the former Soviet Union and the legacy of the Cold War after the collapse of the Soviet Union; prosperity in the Western nations; the relationship between the rich nations and the poor nations; and the ideas and beliefs people in the West find important. We look at the role that modern technology plays in our world, and we consider whether technology can be used to create a good life for all people. Modern technology permits us to do much that is good (prevent disease, improve living standards) and much that is bad (develop nuclear weapons, ruin the natural environment).

Chapter 1, "The Cold War and Its Legacy," discusses the antagonism between the United States and the former Soviet Union that developed after World War II and the nuclear arms race that resulted. One legacy of the Cold War was the collapse of communism in the Soviet Union and the Eastern European nations in the late 1980s and the early 1990s as well as the disintegration of the Soviet Union.

In Chapter 2, "The Wealthy Nations," we discuss the affluence (and its political and social consequences) that the Western nations have enjoyed since World War II. The nations of North America, Western Europe, and Japan, most of which are political democracies, have experienced a level of prosperity almost unparalleled in world history. But Western prosperity has been based on the consumption of enormous amounts of natural resources. In the near future, some resources may become scarce, and already much of the environment has been polluted by industrial production. Some people in Western societies have recently begun to consider how to create economies which provide everyone with a decent material life but consume fewer resources and pollute less.

The third chapter is "The Developing Nations and the Poor Nations." We examine the relationship between the rich countries of the industrialized world (predominantly in Europe and North America) and the poorer nations of Asia, Africa, and Latin America. Are the rich nations obligated to help the poor nations and the rich in a society to help the poor? Over the last few decades, Western societies have given economic development aid and humanitarian assistance to the poor nations and have approved welfare legislation to help the poor in their own countries.

The fourth chapter, "Intellectual and Spiritual Issues in a Technological Age," is about the search for ideas and beliefs that can guide people to a good life. An important part of this chapter is the discussion of the growing influence of religious beliefs and ethical ideas in Western societies. Another significant part of this chapter is the discussion of the transforming power of the Third Industrial Revolution, which is fundamentally altering the ways people live, work, and think.

CHAPTER 1

The Cold War and Its Legacy

INTRODUCTION

Conflicts among the most powerful nations produced arms races, major wars and revolutions, and the deaths of tens of millions of people in the first half of the twentieth century. From 1914 to 1918 Europeans fought World War I, the major combatants being Great Britain, France, Russia, and eventually the United States on one side and Germany and the Hapsburg (Austro-Hungarian) Empire on the other. Between eight and ten million people died as a result of the war. Furthermore, the war undermined several old empires. In 1917 two revolutions shook the Russian Empire, the first overthrowing the tsarist monarchy that had dominated Russia for centuries and the second bringing to power the first communist government in modern history. Then, from 1918 to 1920 the centuries-old Hapsburg Empire disintegrated, and in its place emerged several new nations in Eastern Europe—Poland, Czechoslovakia, Yugoslavia, Austria, Hungary, Rumania, and Bulgaria. At the same time, the Ottoman Empire also disintegrated, and in its place appeared the new nation of Turkey as well as several semi-independent Arab states such as Egypt, Iraq, Saudi Arabia, Syria, Transjordan, and Palestine. (Most Arabic areas remained under the control of European colonial powers until after the Second World War.)

The world was relatively peaceful in the 1920s, but the 1930s saw renewed warfare and large-scale violence. In the Soviet Union (the new communist-designated name for the Russian Empire), the communist dictator Joseph Stalin enforced economic modernization programs in an attempt to rapidly increase Soviet power. Many Soviet citizens resisted these programs, but Stalin and his supporters destroyed the resistance through government-induced famines, mass murders, and a huge labor camp system. As many as twenty million Soviets died in Stalin's modernization campaign.

World War II began to develop in 1937. Japan, seeking to build an Asian empire, invaded China, thus initiating a conflict that lasted until 1945. In 1938 Adolf Hitler's Nazi Germany, allied with fascist Italy, began to seize territories in Eastern Europe. The German invasion of Poland in 1939 began World War II in Europe, because Great Britain and France feared German domination of Europe and resisted German aggressiveness. The war expanded into a massive global conflict in 1941 with the German invasion of the Soviet Union and the Japanese attack on Pearl Harbor, which brought the United States into the war. After 1941 the major combatants were Germany, Italy, and Japan on one side and Great Britain, the Soviet Union, and the United States on the other.

The war in Europe ended in May 1945 with the surrender of Germany and Italy. The war in Asia ended in August 1945. On August 6 an American bomber dropped an atomic bomb on the Japanese city of Hiroshima, killing over a hundred thousand people. Hiroshima was later described as a "graveyard with not a tombstone standing."[1] Three days later a second atomic bomb was dropped on the city of Nagasaki, and within a few more days Japan formally surrendered to the United States. The destruction of Hiroshima and Nagasaki was both the last act of World War II and the first act of the nuclear age.

Approximately 60 million people died as a result of World War II. The Soviet Union suffered the greatest losses, with 20 million military and civilian deaths. The Nazis murdered over 11 million people whom they considered to be "inferior," including 6 million Jews. (The Nazi murder of European Jews later became known as the Holocaust.) In Asia the war was responsible for the deaths of 10 million Chinese and 2.5 million Japanese.

After 1945 two superpowers—the United States and the Soviet Union—dominated world politics, and the history of the relationship between these two nations is the main subject of the chapter.* From the late 1940s into the 1980s the two nations engaged in a global power struggle known as the Cold War and a nuclear arms race in which they accumulated enough nuclear weapons to destroy every person on the planet several times over. In the 1970s and 1980s, however, the world situation changed significantly. The

---

*The term *superpower* refers to the United States and the Soviet Union, the two nations that had powerful nuclear arsenals.

United States, though still the most influential nation on earth, experienced economic problems and a gradual loss of political power in some parts of the world. The Soviet Union, suffering from economic stagnation and political divisions, disintegrated and ceased to exist in the early 1990s, with separate republics breaking away to form independent nations. Also by the 1990s Japan and a unified Germany were major economic powers, winning world influence through industrial production rather than by military conquest as they had attempted to do in World War II.

THE COLD WAR AND THE NUCLEAR ARMS RACE

The Cold War was a worldwide struggle for power between the United States and the Soviet Union. It never resulted in direct military conflict between the two superpowers, but it did lead to competition on all fronts: ideological, diplomatic, economic, and military. Each nation felt besieged by the other. The Soviet leaders came to fear encirclement by capitalist nations and to interpret all American actions as part of a long-range plan to destroy Soviet communism, while the Americans believed that the Soviet Union was bent on world domination.

The power struggle had deep roots, one of which was that geography and history encouraged the two nations to understand international politics in different ways. The world looks different from the perspective of Washington, D.C., than it does from that of Moscow. From Washington, American leaders look out on a nation that throughout its history has been protected from much of the world by two moats—the Atlantic and Pacific oceans. Consequently, Americans have rarely felt threatened by other nations and have come to believe that war only occasionally interrupts the natural cooperation among nations.

From Moscow, the world looks quite different. Russia is located in the middle of a large Eurasian landmass, with Europeans on the western frontier and Asians in the south and east. With all these peoples competing for land and power, Russian history is a record of chronic warfare in which the Russians have been both the attackers and the attacked. As a result, Soviet leaders tended to assume that competition among nations was inevitable and that a nation's security was always precarious.[2]

Another source of the power struggle was the Bolshevik Revolution of 1917 by which a communist party took control of Russia (soon renamed the Soviet Union). According to communist theory, revolution was the order of the day, both within nations and on the international level. In 1918–1919 the new Soviet government hoped that working-class revolutions would overthrow capitalist governments in European countries, but that hope did not materialize. More broadly, the Soviets hoped that a global revolution by the poor, colonized nations (primarily in Asia and Africa) would overthrow the international power and wealth of the rich capitalist nations (mainly the United States and the nations of Western Europe). Since the Soviet Union offered to lead such a global revolution, communist ideas were for a time popular among many Asians and Africans.

The communist call for revolution frightened the United States and the European powers, which saw communism as a militant threat to democracy and capitalism. From 1918 to 1920 several nations, principally Great Britain and France but also the United States, sought unsuccessfully to help Russian conservatives overthrow the communist regime. American fear was so great that not until 1933 did the United States grant diplomatic recognition to the Soviet Union. By the 1940s, however, the Americans and Soviets discovered a common interest in opposing German power in Europe, and they were allied against Germany during World War II. For a time, a spirit of genuine cooperation existed, but there were also disagreements. Allied leaders (Joseph Stalin of the Soviet Union, Franklin D. Roosevelt and then Harry S Truman of the United States, Winston Churchill and then Clement Attlee of Great Britain) met at three summit conferences held in Teheran in November–December 1943, in Yalta in February 1945, and in Potsdam in July–August 1945. Sharp quarrels occurred often at these conferences, some of the primary issues being when the British and Americans would establish a second front against Hitler's Germany, how Germany would be treated after being defeated, and who could control Eastern Europe after Germany's defeat.

After the war the United States and the Soviet Union—the new superpowers—tried to cooperate for a time. Negotiations on some points—how to deal with defeated Japan, for example—were handled relatively amicably. Furthermore, both superpowers participated in the San Francisco conference of April–June 1945, which formally established the United Nations, an international organization designed to maintain world peace through international cooperation.

Cold War in Europe

By 1947 growing hostility between the superpowers was beginning to overwhelm their efforts at cooperation. The immediate source of contention was a series of events in Eastern Europe, particularly in Poland. For the Soviet Union, Poland was an issue of vital national security because three times in this century hostile armies had used Poland as an invasion route into Soviet territory (Germany in World War I and World War II and Poland immediately after World War I). Traditional Russian-Polish antipathy guaranteed that an independent Poland would be hostile to the Soviet Union. Consequently, the Soviets were determined to control Poland. So as Soviet armies pursued German forces across Europe in 1944 and 1945, they brought in their wake a new communist leadership for that country and for the other Eastern European nations as well.

Soviet control of the area developed gradually. In 1945 governmental coalitions including communists and noncommunists were set up in most of the Eastern European states. By 1947 the noncommunists had been pushed out, and communist governments

Europe, 1945–1955: The Cold War

under Soviet domination controlled Poland, Rumania, Bulgaria, Hungary, and the Soviet zone of Germany. In 1948 Czechoslovakia also became fully communist. In a seventh nation, Yugoslavia, a more independent communist government developed after the Yugoslav communist leader Josip Broz Tito repudiated Soviet leadership in 1948.

To most people in the United States and Western Europe, the Soviet actions in Eastern Europe appeared to be aggressive and undemocratic. As a result, between 1945 and 1947 the democratic nations began to perceive the Soviet Union as a hostile expansionist power.* This perception was intensified in a February 1946 speech by Joseph Stalin, wherein the Soviet dictator said that his country had to remain prepared for a possible future war with the capitalist nations. A month later, in another famous speech, Winston Churchill, former wartime prime minister of Great Britain, declared that an "iron curtain" had fallen between Eastern and Western Europe and proposed creation of an Anglo-American alliance against the Soviets.

The next year, when Greece and Turkey were threatened by communist takeovers, President Harry S Truman requested that the American Congress grant economic aid to assist noncommunist governments in those countries. On March 12, 1947, Truman stated in a speech to Congress that "it must be the policy of the United States to support free peoples who are resisting attempted subjugation by armed minorities or by outside pressures."[3] He portrayed the world as divided into two camps, one democratic and the other oppressive and tyrannical, and described a struggle between the two. Congress approved what became known as the "Truman Doctrine" and sent the requested aid to Greece and Turkey. This action marked the real beginning of a new American foreign policy, known as *containment*, meaning that the United States would take the lead in "containing" communist expansion.

The new policy was quickly applied in Western Europe. None of the European nations had recovered from the effects of World War II, and the Americans feared that communist forces would take advantage of the chaos and seize power in some West-

---

*We call the nations of Western Europe and North America the democratic nations because most of them adhere to such basic democratic practices as free and open elections and public debate of major political issues. Some of these nations—Spain, Portugal, Greece—were not democratic during the 1950s and 1960s, but they developed democratic political systems during the 1970s. Some Eastern European nations and some nations that were formerly part of the Soviet Union began to develop democratic systems in the 1990s.

ern European nations. In June 1947 General George C. Marshall, the American secretary of state, proposed a vast program of American economic aid to assist in the economic recovery of Europe. The Marshall Plan, as it was called, funneled large amounts of aid into Western Europe and was instrumental in restoring Western European nations to economic health and political stability. Both the Soviet Union and the Eastern European states refused to participate, since participation would in effect mean adopting a noncommunist economic system.

The effect of these actions of 1945 to 1947 was to divide Europe into two halves, an American-led western half and a Soviet-dominated eastern half, and to increase suspicion and distrust on both sides. In 1948 the suspicion and distrust almost erupted into warfare over the problem of how to deal with Germany. The Nazi government had been destroyed in the last days of World War II, and the Allies had decided that after the war Germany would be occupied briefly by the victorious powers. The United States, the Soviet Union, Great Britain, and France each occupied a section of Germany and were members of an Allied Control Council that was supposed to ensure cooperation among the four occupiers. Berlin, the former German capital, had a special status. Although it was located within the Soviet zone of occupation, Berlin was divided into four sectors, each controlled by one of the occupying powers. Joint administration of the city was to be provided by a committee of representatives from the four powers.

Despite all the well-meaning plans for cooperation, the superpowers found it increasingly difficult to work together in Germany. The lack of cooperation hindered German economic recovery, so the Western powers decided to merge their occupation zones in an attempt to encourage economic development. In 1947 the American and British zones combined into a Bizonia, and in 1948 the French zone was added to form a Trizone economic administration.

The Soviets, convinced that these moves were a prelude to formation of an independent West German state which could threaten them in the future, tried to force the other three nations out of Berlin by establishing a blockade of all roads, railways, and canals leading to the city. The Berlin Blockade, begun in June 1948, prevented all land and sea deliveries of food, fuel, and medical supplies—everything that the city needed to survive. For a time it appeared that the confrontation over Berlin might lead to armed conflict, but both sides acted with care. The United States, Great Britain, and France launched the Berlin Airlift to supply the besieged city by flying over the blockade. The Soviets did not interfere with the Airlift, and eleven months later, in May 1949, the blockade was quietly lifted. In September 1949, a West German state, the Federal Republic of Germany, was formed, and later in the same year an East German state, the German Democratic Republic, was established under Soviet control.

Even as the Berlin crisis eased, in 1949 other developments intensified the superpower conflict. On April 4, 1949, the *N*orth *A*tlantic *T*reaty *O*rganization (NATO) was established to meet any Soviet attack on Western Europe. Members were the United States, Great Britain, France, Belgium, the Netherlands, Luxemburg, Canada, Norway, Iceland, Denmark, Portugal, and Italy. Greece, Turkey, and West Germany joined within a few years, and over three decades later Spain also became a member. In 1955 the Soviet Union organized a counterpart to NATO in the form of the Warsaw Pact, a military alliance between the Soviet Union and the communist states of Eastern Europe.

In 1949 the Soviet Union tested its first atomic bomb. Since both superpowers now had atomic weapons, a nuclear arms race was almost inevitable. In the long history of the world great nations have competed with each other in a variety of ways, but in 1949 began the most dangerous competition of them all. For the next several decades, the paramount issue of international politics would be preventing the superpower conflict from erupting into nuclear war.

The Communist Victory in China

In 1949 and 1950 two events in Asia globalized the superpower conflict. The first event was the communist victory in the Chinese civil war; the second was the Korean War.

The story of China in the twentieth century is that of an ancient nation experiencing a political and social revolution. In 1911 to 1912 a nationalist movement known as the Guomindong (Kuomintang)* overthrew the corrupt, reactionary Manchu dynasty, but the Guomindong was unable to bring stable government to China.

By the late 1920s a struggle for control of China broke out between the Guomindong, now headed by Jiang Jieshi (Chiang Kai-shek), and the Chinese communists, led by Mao Zedong (Mao Tse-tung). The Guomindong was originally stronger, but it became

---

*The spelling of Chinese names has been changed in recent years. For a fuller explanation, and for a discussion of Chinese history since 1949, see the section on China in Chapter 3.

too conservative and too corrupt to retain the loyalty of the Chinese peasantry. By promising land reform for the peasants, Mao and the communists gained the support of the masses. With the end of World War II full-scale civil war broke out in China. Jiang and the Guomindong received political and economic aid from the United States, but they had lost popular support, and in 1949 the communists attained complete control of China. The American-supported Jiang and his armies took refuge on the island of Taiwan, a former Chinese colony.

The communist accession to power in China frightened many people in the United States and Western Europe, because it appeared that world communism was gaining more adherents every day. Russia had become communist in 1917; Eastern Europe, from 1945 to 1947; and China, the most heavily populated country on earth, in 1949. The United States in particular was more determined than ever to block further communist expansion, and the opportunity arose in 1950 in Korea.

The Korean War

A small country surrounded by powerful neighbors (China, Japan, and what was then the Soviet Union), Korea was dominated by Japan during the first half of the twentieth century. When Japanese troops left Korea at the end of World War II, the United Nations assumed responsibility there and designated the Soviet Union to administer the northern half of the country, and the United States the southern half. The administration was supposed to be temporary, as the United Nations planned to sponsor elections for a national government which would reunify Korea. On June 25, 1950, however, North Korea, with Soviet support, launched a surprise attack on South Korea in an effort to accomplish reunification by force.[4] Technically, the North Korean invasion was an attack on the United Nations, and the UN Security Council voted to support South Korea. A United Nations army, composed primarily of Americans (who believed they were leading the global struggle against communism) and commanded by American General Douglas MacArthur, was commissioned to aid South Korea.

At first the North Koreans were successful, but by late 1950 the UN army not only drove them back but launched a counterinvasion of North Korea. When the UN army approached the Korean-Chinese border, Chinese forces joined the battle in support of North Korea. For the next two years the war was a bloody stalemate. Not until 1953 did the two opposing forces conclude an armistice. At that

**General Douglas MacArthur in his jeep at Yangyang, Korea, five miles
north of the 38th parallel, April 3, 1951. Seated in the back (left) are Lt.
Gen. Matthew Ridgway, 8th Army commander, and Maj. Gen. Doyle H.
Skey, acting chief of staff, Far East Command.**

SOURCE: AP/Wide World Photos.

point North and South Korea remained separated by essentially the
same boundary line that had existed in 1950, so the UN forces could
at least say they had maintained the independence of South Korea.

After 1953 South Korea began to achieve significant economic
development and gradually became one of the more prosperous
Asian nations. North Korea remained under the control of communist dictator Kim Il Sung, until he died in 1994 and was succeeded
by his son, Kim Jong Il. In the early 1990s the North Koreans were
suspected of trying to develop nuclear weapons.

The Arms Race and Cold War Tensions

The events in China and Korea increased the tensions between the
superpowers, and both began to make strenuous efforts to protect
themselves. One source of protection was military alliances with

other nations. The Soviets had gained a new ally in China and continued to search for other friends in Asia and Africa. The United States developed formal alliances with a large number of countries, particularly in the Pacific Ocean area and in Asia. By the late 1950s the United States had military agreements with forty-two nations and was obligated under certain conditions to furnish military support to all of them.[5]

Another source of protection was increasing armaments. During the 1950s weapons development and testing expanded on both sides. The hydrogen bomb, which can be anywhere from twenty-five to a thousand times more destructive than the 1945 atomic bombs, was first tested by the United States in 1952 and by the Soviet Union in 1953.

On October 4, 1957, the Soviets launched *Sputnik*, the first space vehicle, and opened up the field of missile development. *Sputnik* was propelled into outer space by powerful rocket engines of the type used to launch nuclear warheads. Very shortly, both the Soviets and the Americans became capable of attacking with missile-launched weapons rather than with cumbersome manned bombers. Missiles were more efficient, faster, and cheaper than bombers. Now wars could start more quickly than before, and people everywhere were more vulnerable than before.[6]

By the early 1960s the Soviet Union had about 100 *i*ntercontinental *b*allistic *m*issiles (ICBMs), and the United States about 550, but each was rapidly developing larger stockpiles of both missiles and warheads.[7] The ever-increasing stockpiles led strategists in both countries to the remarkable conclusion that these weapons could never be used because in actual war neither side could be confident that it would destroy all the enemy's forces. Consequently, since only a few well-aimed nuclear weapons would wreak havoc, there seemed to be no way for one nation to attack the other without itself being demolished by a retaliatory attack.

Standard military strategy came to be the doctrine of deterrence, that is, the doctrine that fear of retaliation would prevent any nation from initiating a nuclear attack. Peace would be maintained by a "balance of terror." (A sobering way of referring to the "balance of terror" is the acronym MAD, or *m*utually *a*ssured *de*struction.) The irony of the arms race was that each of the superpowers constructed huge nuclear arsenals primarily to prevent the other side from using its weapons.[8]

The general public began to awaken to the implications of the arms race when, in 1954, some Japanese fishermen were dusted with radioactive fallout from an American bomb being tested in the Pacific Ocean area. This radiation exposure was at least partly responsible for the death of one of the fishermen,[9] and there was an immediate public outcry about the dangers of fallout.

The fallout debate intensified the growing public fear of nuclear war, which manifested itself in a variety of ways. In both the Soviet Union and the United States, schoolchildren practiced air-raid drills to be prepared in case of nuclear attack. In the United States a novel about the aftermath of nuclear war, *On the Beach*, by Nevil Shute, became a bestseller and was made into a film. American manufacturers developed fallout shelters, underground shelters which were supposed to enable the inhabitants to survive a nuclear war. One enterprising company advertised a $3,000 shelter called the "Mark I Kidde Kokoon," which included a portable radio, air blower, first aid kit, Sterno stove, radiation charts, protective apparel suits, chemical toilet, gasoline-driven generator, pick and shovel for digging out after the blast, and everything needed for a family of five to spend three to five days underground.[10]

The superpowers were obsessively fearful of each other. Each was convinced that it was caught in a struggle for survival that required not only military preparedness but economic and ideological competition as well. Each suspected that spies and enemies were everywhere. Such suspicions and fears deeply affected both countries.

The Soviet Union had been a tightly controlled, closed society for a long time, but Cold War tensions encouraged the Soviet government to become even more repressive. Stalin, the ever-suspicious dictator, feared that too many Soviet citizens had been exposed to foreign influences during World War II and decided that a postwar "rehabilitation" of the Soviet people was in order. Contact between ordinary Soviets and citizens of other countries was prohibited. Any criticism of the Soviet system was outlawed. Disclosure of state secrets—which included all information about Soviet politics, the economy, and the military—was branded as traitorous. An elaborate propaganda campaign gave exaggerated credit to Russians for all sorts of scientific discoveries, including the steam engine, the electric light, and the radio, all of which were discovered by Americans and Europeans. Western art and literature were declared decadent.[11]

Most oppressive were the labor camps designed to isolate and punish anyone suspected of lack of enthusiasm for the Soviet regime. In *The Gulag Archipelago* Aleksandr Solzhenitsyn reports that Soviet citizens sent to the labor camps included civilians who had lived in German-occupied Russia during the war, soldiers who had been prisoners of war, Russian women who had fraternized with foreigners, alleged spies, religious believers, and anyone who praised American democracy and technology.

No one really knows how many people went to the camps, but Solzhenitsyn believes that the number of camp inmates was as high as twelve million at one time. People sent to the camps spent ten or more years at hard physical labor in a bitterly cold climate (see the discussion on Solzhenitsyn in Chapter 4). Many did not survive. If they did, there was always the chance of being interrogated under torture. Solzhenitsyn testifies that some prisoners had their skulls squeezed with iron rings, some were lowered into acid baths, some had red-hot ramrods thrust up their anal canals, some men had their genitals crushed by the guards' boots, while the more fortunate were tortured by being deprived of food and water or by being beaten.[12]

Nothing as brutal as the Soviet labor camps existed in the United States, but Cold War tensions produced some changes in American government and society. One result was the gradual evolution of what scholars came to call the "national security state," which required organizing all American institutions, both public and private, to protect national security.[13] The most prominent feature of the national security state was what President Dwight D. Eisenhower called the "military-industrial complex," a loose grouping of institutions whose purpose was to do research and develop new weapons for national defense. The military-industrial complex included the armed forces, many private business firms and universities doing weapons research, and several "think tanks" where scholars explored nuclear strategy as well as weapons development. (The Soviet Union undoubtedly had a military-industrial complex of its own, so both nations had powerful institutional forces devoted to weapons research and development.)

Another result of the tensions of the time was the spy scare of the late 1940s. Although the spy scare was greatly exaggerated, many Americans came to believe that communists had infiltrated the U.S. government. The person who capitalized the most on the spy scare was Senator Joseph McCarthy of Wisconsin. Early in 1950 McCarthy claimed that there were fifty-seven known communists in the State Department. He was vague when it came to naming the people, but for the next several years he created a national furor by continually charging that communists were scattered throughout the American government. Eventually, McCarthy overreached himself by appearing to attack the U.S. military, and in 1954 his influence ended when the Senate voted to condemn his actions. By then, however, he had wrecked many people's public and professional careers.

A poignant example of the tensions of the times is the case of Robert Oppenheimer, the brilliant scientist who directed the American-British research project that produced the first atomic bomb. After World War II Oppenheimer continued to advise the government on nuclear energy, but he gradually came under suspicion for a number of reasons. For one thing he opposed the development of the hydrogen bomb. Also, some of his friends had belonged to the Communist party during the 1930s and 1940s. The political pressure of McCarthyism was such that in 1954 the *Atomic Energy Commission* (AEC) declared Oppenheimer to be a loyal citizen but a security risk and barred him from further access to government secrets. From then on, his reputation was tarnished.

Slow Easing of Cold War Tensions

Clearly, the Cold War placed a heavy burden on both superpowers—not only in the enormous financial costs of weapons and military alliances but also in the tensions that afflicted ordinary American and Soviet citizens. Both nations had much to gain if international hostilities could be eased, and the first opportunity to do so occurred in 1953, when two of the protagonists of the Cold War left the scene.

In the United States President Harry S Truman chose not to run for reelection and was replaced by the American war hero Dwight D. Eisenhower. In March 1953 Joseph Stalin died, and soon it became apparent that the dominant voice in the new Soviet leadership was that of Nikita Khrushchev.

Both Eisenhower and Khrushchev were interested in moderating international tensions. Indeed, Eisenhower seemed to summarize the feelings of the two men when he said in the spring of 1953: "Both their government and ours now have new men in them. The slate is clean. Now let us begin talking to each other."[14]

Over the next two or three years several developments indicated that Soviet-American relations were improving slightly. One was the Geneva Conference of 1955, the first summit conference since World War II. The Geneva Conference accomplished little, but it demonstrated that the leaders of the most powerful nations on earth were trying to talk with each other. Another was the signing of the Austrian State Treaty in 1955. Austria had been occupied by Soviet, American, British, and French forces since the end of the war, but the 1955 treaty finally resolved Austria's status. Austria was declared a neutral state, and the occupation troops were removed.

The third development was Khrushchev's 1956 secret speech to the Twentieth Congress of the Soviet Communist party. His speech was a long denunciation of Joseph Stalin. Khrushchev was an enthusiastic communist, but he thought that Stalin had governed far too harshly and that the excesses of Stalinist totalitarianism had to be eradicated. The content of the speech soon became known both in the Soviet Union and throughout the rest of the world. Khrushchev's denunciation of Stalin moderated Cold War fears because it eased the political and social tensions within the Soviet Union, in much the same way that the American Senate's condemnation of Joseph McCarthy eased tensions in the United States.

The slight improvement in superpower relations was interrupted by two international crises in 1956. The first was in Eastern Europe, where Khrushchev's speech had the unintended effect of helping to precipitate Polish and Hungarian revolts against Soviet domination. In Poland a nationalist communist named Wladyslaw Gomulka came to power, and for a time it appeared that Poland would seek independence from Soviet control. A compromise with the Soviets was worked out, though, and the Polish crisis eased.

A greater challenge to Soviet leadership occurred in Hungary, where another nationalist communist, Imre Nagy, took power. In November 1956 Nagy announced that Hungary would end its alliance with the Soviet Union and pursue a neutralist foreign policy. That was more than the Soviets could tolerate, and Soviet tanks moved into Hungary to crush the rebellion. Nagy and a number of his supporters were executed, and Hungary remained under Soviet control.

The Soviets were fortunate that the international furor created by their crushing of the Hungarian rebellion was overshadowed by a crisis in the Middle East over the Suez Canal, a waterway through Egyptian territory which provides the shortest sea route between Europe and Asia. Great Britain had long controlled the canal, but under Egyptian pressure withdrew its troops from the canal zone in 1954 and 1955. In 1956 President Gamal Abdel Nasser of Egypt nationalized the canal. Determined to regain control of this commercially vital waterway, Britain and France collaborated with Israel, which was hostile to Egypt because the Egyptians supported the Arab desire to destroy the Israeli state. (See Chapter 3 for the Arab-Israeli conflict. Both Palestinian Arabs and Israelis claim the same area as their homeland, the result being chronic hostility and occasional warfare between the two.) On October 29, 1956, the three nations launched an invasion of Egypt and were immediately successful, but the invasion set off a storm of protests around the world. Many Asian and African nations saw the invasion as a revival of colonial conquest, and the United States condemned the invasion for the same reason even though the invaders were American allies. The invaders were forced to withdraw, and the Suez crisis ended. When the fighting was over, Egypt retained control of the canal, and British and French colonial power in the Middle East never recovered.

The crises of 1956 and the launching of *Sputnik* in 1957, which increased superpower rivalry, made it difficult for the superpowers to continue their efforts at cooperation. Nevertheless, Eisenhower and Khrushchev sought ways to improve relations between their countries, and in September 1959 Khrushchev became the first Soviet leader to visit the United States. Because he acted like a tourist and even lunched with movie stars in Hollywood, Khrushchev created a sensation in the American press. Far more important were the talks he and Eisenhower held at the presidential retreat at Camp David, Maryland. For a time the "spirit of Camp David" seemed to signal a new era of Soviet-American cooperation and even friendship.

The two leaders planned to meet again at a Paris summit conference in May 1960. Two weeks before the conference, however, the Soviets shot down an American U-2 reconnaissance plane that had been flying over the Soviet Union to gather military intelligence. Khrushchev complained vociferously about American spying, and when Eisenhower refused to "punish" the U-2 "culprits," the Soviet leader walked out of the Paris meeting.

Thus, the superpower relationship remained turbulent when Eisenhower left office in 1960. Yet he and Khrushchev had succeeded in moderating the more extreme hostilities of the early Cold War and paving the way for some superpower cooperation in later decades.

1960s: MAJOR SUPERPOWER PROBLEMS AND CRISES

In the 1960s a series of major problems and crises—the Sino-Soviet split, the Berlin Wall, the Cuban missile crisis, and the Vietnam War—afflicted the superpowers. The Sino-Soviet split was primarily a Soviet problem, and the Vietnam War an American problem; the Berlin Wall and the Cuban missile crisis involved both superpowers. This series of problems and crises heightened international tensions, but they also encouraged the superpowers to seek *détente*, or "relaxation of tensions."

The Sino-Soviet Split

The Sino-Soviet split refers to the collapse of the alliance between the two major communist nations, the Soviet Union and China. During the years since the Chinese communists came to power in 1949, the nations appeared to be working harmoniously. But in 1960 they began to denounce each other in public. Shortly afterward the Soviets recalled their technicians, who had been sent to help China industrialize. One Chinese newspaper called the Russians "filthy Soviet revisionist swine."

There were several reasons for the conflict between the Russians and the Chinese. One was a long-standing dispute over territory along the 4,500 miles of their shared border. Another reason was that China challenged the Soviets for leadership of the world communist movement. A third was that the Chinese accused the Soviets of giving up the struggle against capitalism by seeking peaceful relations with the United States. Finally, the Soviets feared that the Chinese would develop nuclear weapons. In fact the Chinese tested their first atomic bomb in 1964, and their first hydrogen bomb in 1967.[15]

Because China borders the Soviet Union, Soviet leaders quickly concluded that China, not the United States, was the more immediate threat to their national security. Consequently, one effect of the Sino-Soviet split was to force the Soviets to improve their relations with the United States, for the simple reason that they did not want to face two implacable enemies at the same time.[16] Soviet leaders particularly feared that China and the United States would begin to cooperate against the Soviet Union. That fear increased after U.S. President Richard M. Nixon visited Beijing in 1972, and the two countries established diplomatic relations in 1979.

The Berlin Wall

Berlin had been a source of superpower conflict since the end of World War II. Periodically, the Soviets pressured the other occupying powers to leave the city and allow it to become part of East Germany. A major reason for the Soviet pressure was the fact that thousands of East Germans were simply walking from East Berlin to West Berlin and then seeking a new home in West Germany or some other country. West Berlin was thus an escape hatch for Germans fleeing the communist regime and a major embarrassment for the Soviet Union. To stop people from leaving, the communists constructed the Berlin Wall in August 1961. It was a concrete barrier separating West from East Berlin which prevented any further emigration of East Germans to the West and divided families who lived in different parts of the city. For the people of Berlin, the Wall was a source of oppression and hardship. In terms of international politics the Wall created a furor, but in the long run it also helped encourage détente. The Soviets no longer felt threatened by the Berlin problem, so Berlin was not a major diplomatic issue between the superpowers after 1961.[17] The Wall was finally dismantled in 1989, when the Soviets relinquished control of East Germany (see discussion later in this chapter).

The Cuban Missile Crisis

The Berlin Wall crisis was minor compared with the Cuban missile crisis of October 1962. In January 1959 Fidel Castro had seized power in Cuba after leading a revolution that overthrew the corrupt dictatorship of General Fulgencio Batista. Castro soon proclaimed himself a communist and in 1960 accepted Soviet military protection for Cuba. The United States, watching with apprehension this new communist nation only ninety miles from the American mainland, broke diplomatic relations with Cuba early in 1961.

Then, in April 1961, a small army of Cuban exiles with American support attempted to invade Cuba at the Bay of Pigs. The exiles hoped that the attack would precipitate an internal uprising against Castro, but the Bay of Pigs invasion ended in disaster, with most of the invading army being killed or captured. By 1962 the United States and Cuba were open enemies.

In October 1962 American intelligence reports revealed that the Soviets were installing missile sites in Cuba from which nuclear warheads could be launched a distance of up to 1,400 miles. Although the warheads had not yet arrived in Cuba, the Soviet installations appeared to threaten American security. (The Americans did not know it at the time, but Soviet troops in Cuba had small battlefield nuclear weapons.)

American President John F. Kennedy declared that a nuclear missile launched from Cuba at the United States would result in retaliation against the Soviet Union, and he established a naval blockade around Cuba to prevent delivery of any Soviet missiles or warheads. For a few days it appeared that this confrontation might lead to war between the superpowers, and Castro did try to persuade Soviet premier Khrushchev to launch a preemptive nuclear strike at the United States. Fortunately, Kennedy and Khrushchev were corresponding directly, and they managed to defuse the crisis. In the end Khrushchev agreed to dismantle the missile sites in exchange for an American pledge not to invade Cuba.

The Cuban missile crisis frightened everyone, including Kennedy and Khrushchev. Consequently, the next year the two leaders agreed to establish a teletype-like hot line between Moscow and Washington, on the assumption that better communications would reduce the possibility of accidental war. Also in 1963 the superpowers concluded a treaty which placed some mild restraints on the arms competition. The nuclear test ban treaty prohibited testing of nuclear weapons in the atmosphere and in the oceans. It was only a partial test ban, since both nations continued to conduct numerous underground tests. In the long run the treaty had little effect on nuclear weapons development, but it led to a reduction of radioactivity in the atmosphere and thus was important as a public health measure.[18]

Nikita Khrushchev did not enjoy the improved relations with the United States for very long. His political position had been undermined by a number of factors, including the Sino-Soviet split, the appearance of Soviet weakness in the Cuban missile crisis, and shortages in agricultural production in the Soviet Union. In October 1964 Khrushchev lost a power struggle within the Soviet hierarchy and was replaced by Leonid Brezhnev and Alexei Kosygin. Over the years Brezhnev emerged as the dominant personality, but he was the leader of a small group of Soviet rulers and not an absolute dictator as Stalin had been. It became evident that the governing group wished to continue a policy of some cooperation with the United States, and Brezhnev gradually began to portray détente as a cornerstone of Soviet foreign policy.

The Vietnam War

By the mid-1960s the United States was becoming militarily involved in a war in Vietnam, an experience that would make détente appear more attractive to American leaders. Vietnam had been a part of the French colony of Indochina since the nineteenth century. During World War II Japan dominated Vietnam, but, when the war was over, France tried to reassert control. Many Vietnamese, however, had joined a national liberation movement directed by the nationalist and communist leader Ho Chi Minh, and in 1946 war broke out between the Vietnamese and the French, who were finally defeated in 1954. In that year the Geneva Conference partitioned Indochina into four countries: Laos, Cambodia, North Vietnam (controlled by Ho Chi Minh), and South Vietnam (supported by American aid).

The two halves of Vietnam were supposed to be unified through election of a national government, but President Ngo Dinh Diem of South Vietnam, fearing that Ho Chi Minh would win, refused to participate in any election. North Vietnam then began, in the late 1950s, to support guerrilla warfare against South Vietnam in an effort to achieve national unification by force. At that point the United States began to be heavily involved. Both Presidents Eisenhower and Kennedy sent supplies and some military advisers to South Vietnam and thereby slowly increased the American commitment. The Americans believed that the struggle in Vietnam was another instance of communist expansion. They feared the broader implications of the Vietnamese conflict because they believed in the "domino theory." According to the theory, if one small nation like South Vietnam fell to the communists, then nearby countries would inevitably follow, like dominoes in a row, until the communists were threatening American shores. The Americans ignored the fact that the North Vietnamese were not only communists but also nationalists fighting for the national freedom of Vietnam. Many Vietnamese perceived all foreign troops, Americans included, as invaders who had to be repulsed.

By 1964–1965 South Vietnam was losing the struggle, so to remedy the situation President Lyndon B. Johnson sent American combat troops to Vietnam in 1965. Over the next few years the conflict escalated until, by the late 1960s, over half a million American troops were in Vietnam. The result was a nightmare for the Americans. The war itself was a guerrilla conflict often fought in junglelike terrain where booby traps and ambush attacks were common. It became a war of attrition, with each side trying to wear the other down. As the years went by, the Americans began to be frustrated by their inability to defeat decisively the North Vietnamese and the Viet Cong guerrilla army in the south. Protest demonstrations against the war erupted on many college campuses in the United States. The feelings of many Americans were expressed by an infantryman in Vietnam who wrote "UUUU" on his helmet. It stood for "The Unwilling, led by the Unqualified, doing the Unnecessary for the Ungrateful."

The most crushing blow for the Americans was the Tet offen-

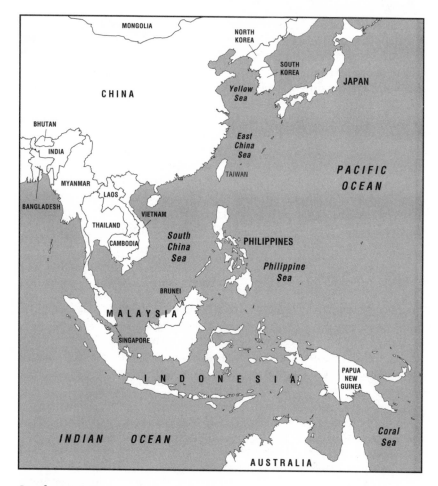

Southeast Asia

sive of January–February 1968, in which the Viet Cong struck at dozens of targets. Militarily, Tet was a defeat for the Viet Cong, but psychologically it was a loss for the Americans because it demonstrated that the Viet Cong could not be overcome quickly and that the U.S. government had exaggerated American progress toward winning the conflict. American public opinion increasingly turned against the war, and so the American government began to seek a negotiated end to the war. But North Vietnam, rightly believing it was winning, was slow to cooperate. The conflict spread to Cambodia in 1970 and to Laos in 1971. The United States finally had to ask the Soviet Union and China to pressure North Vietnam to go to the negotiating table, and eventually a peace agreement was concluded. The last American combat troops left Vietnam in 1973; and the last American government officials departed in 1975, although some people believe that a few American soldiers remained captive in Southeast Asian prisons (as the years go by, this seems less likely).

In 1975 North Vietnam completed its victory by overrunning all of South Vietnam and soon thereafter gaining effective control of Cambodia and Laos as well. For the United States the Vietnam conflict was a humbling experience, because not only did the Americans lose the war but they also required the help of two old adversaries, the Soviet Union and China, in order to get out of the war. Thus, one result of the Vietnam War was to force the United States to seek better relations with both communist powers.

1970s: DÉTENTE

The French word *détente*, meaning "relaxation of tensions," was the term used to describe a new era in Soviet-American relations that began in the late 1960s and lasted to the late 1970s. Détente was a major effort to control the nuclear arms race and moderate some of the conflicts of the Cold War.

Arms Control

Arms control was at first the most important feature of détente. The first step occurred in 1968, when a nuclear nonproliferation treaty was adopted. *Proliferation* refers to the fact that more and more countries were acquiring the ability to construct nuclear weapons. The 1968 treaty sought to stop weapons expansion by allowing those nations which already possessed nuclear weapons (the United States, the Soviet Union, Britain, France, China) to keep them. Countries without nuclear weapons would be required to accept international inspection of their nuclear installations to ensure that nuclear energy would be used only for peaceful purposes. Because of this restriction and because some nations were allowed to retain nuclear weapons, a number of important countries (Argentina, Brazil, India, Israel, Egypt, Spain, Pakistan, and South Africa) refused to sign the treaty. As a result, the treaty was not completely effective.[19] (In 1993–1994 North Korea withdrew from the treaty, possibly because it was constructing an atomic bomb.)

In 1969 the SALT (*S*trategic *A*rms *L*imitations *T*alks) negotiations began, and in 1972 a SALT I agreement was concluded by President Richard Nixon of the United States (aided by Secretary of State Henry Kissinger) and Leonid Brezhnev of the Soviet Union. By this treaty the superpowers, believing their nuclear arsenals were of roughly equivalent size, agreed to freeze the number of their strategic weapons for five years. (*Strategic* weapons are those which have an intercontinental range and thus could be used by either superpower to strike directly at the other. *Tactical* weapons have a shorter range.) At the time the Soviets had 1,618 intercontinental *b*allistic *m*issiles (ICBMs) based on land and 740 *s*ubmarine-*l*aunched *b*allistic *m*issiles (SLBMs), while the United States had 1,054 missiles on land and 656 on submarines, in addition to weapons carried on manned bombers.[20]

The freeze on offensive weapons had only limited effectiveness. One problem was that SALT I restricted only the number of launchers and not the number of warheads (the bombs themselves); nothing prevented either nation from equipping their missiles with multiple warheads. Also, the SALT agreement placed no restrictions on *qualitative* improvements of either missiles or warheads. Even though SALT I placed some limits on the arms race, there was still plenty of room for arms competition.[21]

Far more important was another part of SALT I, a treaty on limitation of *a*nti*b*allistic *m*issile (ABM) systems. In the 1960s both superpowers began to develop antiballistic missiles, which could theoretically shoot attacking missiles out of the sky and protect a nation from nuclear attack.

ABM was an idea that sounded better in theory than in practice, since a really effective ABM system would have to be virtually perfect. Even if a nation's ABM system destroyed almost all attacking missiles, the few bombs that got through would cause tremendous destruction. Nuclear weapons are so powerful that there is no margin for error in an ABM system.[22] The SALT I agreement recognized that there was no effective defense against offensive nuclear weapons and limited the superpowers to two and later to one ABM site. In the end, the ABM treaty was the most effective arms control agreement concluded in the 1970s.

Other treaties soon followed the SALT I agreement. In May 1972 the superpowers signed an accord in which they pledged to work for "peaceful coexistence." Then, in June 1973, they concluded an agreement that obligated them to consult urgently whenever an international crisis threatened to erupt into nuclear war. And, in the late 1970s a SALT II agreement was concluded, although it was never formally approved.

Détente in Europe

Détente had a major impact in Europe. Early in the 1970s Willy Brandt, the West German chancellor, implemented a new foreign policy called *Ostpolitik* (East politics). This policy resulted in West German nonaggression treaties with Poland, the Soviet Union, and East Germany. The effect of the treaties was to settle a number of territorial disputes left over from World War II and thereby ease tensions in Central Europe. In particular, *Ostpolitik* resulted in allowing some West Germans to visit relatives in East Germany, the first free movement of people across the common German border since construction of the Berlin Wall.

The culmination of détente was the 1975 Conference on Security and Cooperation in Europe, which was held in Helsinki, Finland, and thus became popularly known as the Helsinki Conference. This conference produced the Helsinki Agreements, by which the two superpowers and thirty-five other nations concluded three major points: (1) a declaration that no European frontiers should be violated, which in effect legalized the frontiers established in 1945; (2) an agreement to encourage trade between Eastern and Western Europe; and (3) a pledge to encourage free movement of people and ideas within and between European nations. In practice, the Helsinki Agreements led to greatly increased trade and communication between the communist and noncommunist parts of Europe.

The era of détente lasted little more than a decade, but at least two important developments occurred during that era. One was that the superpowers reduced Cold War tensions and concluded some arms control measures. The other was that some aspects of détente, particularly West German *Ostpolitik* and the Helsinki Agreements, opened the communist nations to some democratic influences and thus helped precipitate the demise of communism in the Soviet Union and Eastern European nations in the late 1980s and early 1990s.

The End of Détente

Détente ended during the late 1970s. From the perspective of the United States, the end of détente was caused by the Soviets. Despite arms control negotiations the Soviets engaged in a sustained military buildup during the 1960s and 1970s. Furthermore, Soviet expansionism seemed to increase during the late 1970s. The Soviets gave political and military support to new Marxist governments in Angola in 1975, Ethiopia in 1977, and Nicaragua after

1979. And, late in 1979, Soviet troops went to Afghanistan to bolster a communist government and remained to fight against the Afghan resistance through the 1980s.

From the Soviet perspective, it was the Americans who destroyed détente. Anticommunist attitudes remained very strong in the United States, and those attitudes helped elect the conservative Ronald Reagan to the American presidency in 1980. Reagan believed that the United States lagged behind in the arms race, so he delayed arms control negotiations and sought to expand the American military arsenal. In particular, he proposed in 1983 the development of what he called the Strategic Defense Initiative (SDI), popularly known as "Star Wars." The principle underlying SDI was the same as that underlying the ABM weapons of the early 1970s, in that SDI was supposed to be a space-based defense system that would protect the United States from nuclear attack. After 1983 the United States started a research program to develop the technology needed for SDI, but in the early 1990s that technology was still in the experimental stage. Nevertheless, the possibility that an SDI system might exist someday worried Soviet leaders. They continually argued that an SDI system would violate the 1972 ABM treaty and escalate the arms race.

Some writers referred to the early 1980s as Cold War II, because the arms race was escalating and the superpower relationship was increasingly hostile. In reality, however, the Cold War was almost over, for in the late 1980s the communist system collapsed, and the Soviet Union began to disintegrate.

1980s: COLLAPSE OF COMMUNISM AND THE DISINTEGRATION OF THE SOVIET UNION

The Stalinist System in the Soviet Union

The Soviet Union had become a major industrial power in the first half of the twentieth century. Joseph Stalin, the Soviet dictator, believed that industrial power had enabled his country to survive the German onslaught during the war. After 1945 Stalin directed that economic reconstruction emphasize redevelopment of heavy industries such as steel and iron and the production of armaments. Because Stalin was determined that the Communist party control everything, the Soviet economic system was a "command economy." Government bureaucrats determined prices and decided where and how to invest capital and how much of an item to produce. Monthly or yearly production quotas had to be met by every industrial enterprise and state-controlled collective farm.

The emphasis on heavy industry and armaments meant that production of consumer goods was deemphasized. The Soviet Union was therefore a major world power whose citizens had a standard of living far lower than that of some less powerful nations. This situation began to change a little after the death of Stalin and the accession of Nikita Khrushchev to power in the late 1950s. The Soviet economic system began to produce more consumer goods, and the standard of living slowly but surely improved. Housing and food subsidies kept basic costs low for most people. Between 1950 and 1970 per capita food consumption doubled. By the early 1970s two-thirds of the nation's families had television sets, nearly 60 percent had washing machines, and about half had some kind of refrigerator.

The Soviet economy slowly stagnated during the 1970s, however. The annual growth rate in industrial production averaged close to 6 percent in the 1950s, but by the early 1980s it was only about 1.5 percent.[23] One reason for the decline was the continual stifling of local initiative by central planners. Another was the high priority given to military production, which absorbed most of the available research funds and trained personnel.

The agricultural system also faltered. During the 1970s the Soviets were forced to import grain for much of the decade because their grain production failed to keep up with demand. The grain shortages occurred partly because much Soviet farmland was in a cold climate, north of the forty-ninth parallel, but also because state-controlled collective farms, where all farmers worked together, inhibited individual initiative and decision-making.

Political torpor accompanied economic stagnation. Nikita Khrushchev was overthrown in 1964 and was replaced by a small ruling elite headed by Leonid Brezhnev. During the Brezhnev years (1964–1982), this ruling elite increasingly became a collection of unimaginative old men unwilling to find any creative solutions to Soviet problems or to allow anyone outside the ruling hierarchy to be creative. Professional, educated people became increasingly disenchanted with the Brezhnev regime. Since World War II the Soviet population had gradually become much more educated and urban, and the new professionals particularly resented government controls on people's ability to travel and communicate with others.[24]

The most obvious sign of this resentment was the emergence

of a dissident movement. In the mid-1960s a small human rights movement began. It was composed at its peak of about two thousand intellectuals who criticized human rights violations by the Soviet government. Since the government tried to silence these intellectuals, they usually published their writings in the form of *samizdat* (illegal typed copies of manuscripts that were circulated clandestinely). When the Helsinki Agreements with their human rights provisions were signed in 1975 by the Soviet government, some Soviet dissidents founded a Helsinki Watch Group to publicize the repressive acts of the government.

Intellectuals were not the only dissenters. National dissident movements, such as those of Ukrainians and Lithuanians, began to seek some degree of political and cultural autonomy. Grassroots ecological groups protested against specific acts of environmental destruction. Religious dissidents—Catholics, Baptists, Pentecostals—resisted government interference in their religious practices. Soviet Jews constantly protested against Soviet unwillingness to allow them to emigrate to Israel and thereby escape Soviet anti-Semitism.

Two of the most famous dissidents were Aleksandr Solzhenitsyn and Andrei Sakharov. Solzhenitsyn exposed the cruelty and inhumanity of the Stalinist labor camp system in books such as *The Gulag Archipelago* and thus helped undermine the historical reputation of Joseph Stalin, the man most responsible for forming the Soviet Union as it existed in the 1970s. (See Chapter 4 for a detailed discussion of Solzhenitsyn's work.) Sakharov, a brilliant scientist who helped build the Soviet hydrogen bomb, argued that intellectual freedom and some form of democratic government were essential to human progress. He constantly criticized the Soviet regime for blocking progress. The government punished both men, sending Solzhenitsyn into exile to the United States. Sakharov, along with his wife and fellow dissident Elena Bonner, was imprisoned in internal exile. Sakharov and Bonner were released by Mikhail Gorbachev in 1986.

The dissident movement never included more than a few thousand activists, but it constituted an important moral opposition to the communist regime. As such, it helped undermine the legitimacy of that regime by continually criticizing the abuses perpetrated by the ruling elites. Furthermore, by insisting on the importance of freedom of thought, the dissident movement began the process of emancipating the Soviet people from the ideological controls imposed by the communist party.

Gorbachev

After Leonid Brezhnev died in 1982, two other old men—Yuri Andropov and Konstantin Chernenko—briefly ruled the Soviet Union in succession, but each died after only a few months in power. In 1985 Mikhail Gorbachev became the dominant figure. Gorbachev was much younger than the previous rulers, a representative of the new professional, educated groups in the Soviet Union. These groups wanted to modernize the Soviet Union so that it could compete in a high-technology world.

Gorbachev was a reform Communist whose first goal was to transform the Soviet economy through *perestroika* (restructuring), which originally meant reorganizing the government bureaucracy to make it more efficient and creating greater quality control of industrial products without basically changing the nature of the state-controlled economy. By 1986 many bureaucrats and communist party members were opposing Gorbachev because they feared the loss of their traditional powers, so he began to call for *glasnost* (openness), a more open debate to create public pressure for economic reforms. The result was unprecedented in Soviet history, for a growing number of people began to discuss and argue about many different issues in newspapers, magazines, and public meeting places. *Glasnost* produced so much criticism of the Soviet system that its credibility was gradually eroded. *Glasnost* also threatened to undermine the country itself, since the Soviet Union contained many different national groups—Lithuanians, Latvians, Georgians, Ukrainians, and others—for whom *glasnost* provided an opportunity to issue demands for autonomy within or independence from the Soviet Union.

By the late 1980s, Gorbachev and his supporters realized that the Soviet Union no longer had the strength and energy to sustain all the components of its international power. Consequently, the Soviet leadership became increasingly willing to negotiate arms control treaties with the United States, both in order to lessen the threat of nuclear war and to decrease the economic burdens imposed by the arms race. In December 1987, Gorbachev and President Reagan signed an INF treaty (*I*ntermediate-range *N*uclear *F*orces), by which both sides agreed to dismantle all their short- and medium-range missiles, most of which were deployed in Europe. Then, in July 1991, Gorbachev and George Bush (who assumed the U.S. presidency in 1989) signed the START I agreement (*S*trategic *A*rms *R*eduction *T*reaty), by which each nation pledged to eliminate about one-third of the nuclear warheads from its strategic arsenal. After the disintegration of the Soviet Union in December 1991, the Soviet nuclear arsenal was in effect divided among four newly independent republics—Russia, Ukraine, Belarus, and Kazakhstan. Russia continued to express support of START, and Belarus and Kazakhstan agreed to relinquish their nuclear weapons, but Ukraine wanted major U.S. economic assistance as compensation for giving up nuclear weapons.

Another consequence of declining Soviet power was the decision to withdraw Soviet military forces from Afghanistan early in 1989, thus ending Soviet intervention in that country. Civil war continued to plague Afghanistan, however, in part because the communist Afghan government remained in power until 1992 and many Afghans strongly opposed that government.

Within the Soviet Union life became increasingly chaotic, as the Communist party slowly lost authority, the economy faltered, food shortages began to develop, and the government seemed incapable of controlling the situation or producing any meaningful reform plans. To bolster his position Gorbachev began to talk about increased democratization of the Soviet system, and in the late 1980s some semi-free elections allowed Soviet citizens a choice in selecting representatives to various political bodies.

The End of the Soviet Union

Political and economic chaos continued, however, and in August 1991 some Communist party leaders, who opposed and feared the reform process, attempted a coup. Gorbachev was briefly removed from power, but the coup collapsed in a few days. Coup leaders were denounced by many street demonstrators, led in Moscow by Boris Yeltsin, head of the Russian Republic, the largest republic in the Soviet Union. This popular resistance to the coup revealed the depth of public support for the reform process. The military was another source of opposition to the coup, as many military units refused to support coup leaders, probably because many officers supported reform in the hope that it would lead to modernization of the armed forces. The collapse of the coup resulted in Gorbachev's being restored to office and the Soviet Communist party's being completely discredited.

By late 1991 the Soviet Union was disintegrating. In that year, the Baltic areas of Lithuania, Latvia, and Estonia wrested their independence from the Soviet Union. As other national groups such as the Ukrainians and the Georgians also threatened to leave, a

President Boris Yeltsin of Russia preparing to shake hands with President Bill Clinton in the Oval Office of the White House, September 27, 1994. President Clinton welcomed Yeltsin saying that the two nations have to move from an era of "mistrust and suspicion" to a period of "trust and cooperation."

Source: Doug Mills/AP/Wide World Photos.

series of negotiations among leaders of the major national groups led to a decision to disband the Soviet Union. The Soviet Union officially ceased to exist on December 25, 1991, and Gorbachev returned to private life. (The irony of Gorbachev's political career was that he meant to reform and thereby strengthen the Soviet Union, but his reform efforts actually helped destroy the Soviet system.) Replacing the defunct Soviet Union was a Commonwealth of Independent States, each state having its own government. The commonwealth was made up of most of the former Soviet constituent republics, most importantly Russia (led by Boris Yeltsin), the Ukraine, and Belarus (Byelorussia).

Thus, in 1992 the peoples of the former Soviet Union began a new era in their history. The new states that were members of the Commonwealth of Independent States had to decide who would control the assets and military forces that had belonged to the Soviet Union. Within the individual states, governments had to develop new political and economic systems to replace the old Soviet systems. However, prolonged civil conflict between ethnic groups plagued some new states, and economic problems such as inflation and unemployment hurt others, particularly Russia. (For a more complete discussion of these topics, see Chapter 2.)

The Stalinist System in the Eastern European Nations

At the end of World War II, backward peasant economies with little modern industry dominated the Eastern European countries (Poland, Czechoslovakia, East Germany, Hungary, Bulgaria, Romania, and Yugoslavia). From 1945 to 1947 governments in most of these countries responded to local desires for social and economic change. Land reform programs destroyed the old estates of the ruling aristocracy and distributed land to many peasants. Key industries were nationalized, a popular move because such industries had usually been owned by foreigners.

Starting in 1947 the Russians asserted more direct control over the Eastern European countries (except for Yugoslavia, which remained free of Soviet control). The Eastern European governments became fully communist, and Soviet-style economic systems were imposed. Most farmland was absorbed into state-owned collectives, provoking strong peasant protests. Trade patterns with Western Europe were broken, and the Soviets began to dominate Eastern European trade. By imposing low prices on Eastern European exports to Russia and high prices on Russian exports to Eastern Europe, the Soviets in effect exacted forced contributions from Eastern Europe for Soviet reconstruction from war damage.

As a result economic development in Eastern Europe was very slow. Peasant grievances, low industrial wages, and shortages of consumer goods gradually produced enormous discontent with Soviet domination. The discontent flared into open revolt with an East Berlin workers' strike in 1953 and the Polish and Hungarian rebellions of 1956.

In the 1960s the lot of the Eastern European consumer slowly began to improve. By the beginning of the 1970s both Czechoslovakia and East Germany achieved a GNP per capita of about $3,000. Hungary stressed production of consumer goods in pursuit of what was called "goulash communism." The other Eastern European states were not quite as wealthy, but they too were progressing.

Life was getting better for many people in Eastern Europe, but the standard of living remained far below that of Western Europe and North America.

The Eastern European countries were hurt by the global recession of the 1970s, during which several communist countries borrowed large sums of money, primarily from private banks in the democratic nations, to pay for increased imports from Western Europe. By the 1980s some of these countries, particularly Poland and Romania, were having difficulty repaying their loans. The result was governmental imposition of major price increases, which increased popular discontent with the communist regimes.

Popular discontent led to unrest. In 1968 several moderate communist leaders, led by Alexander Dubček, came to power in Czechoslovakia and with much popular support began to introduce political and social reforms. The Soviets, fearful of this turn of events, sent troops in to remove the moderate communists and reimpose a Stalinist, hard-line government. Another example of unrest were the religious revivals that developed in Poland, Czechoslovakia, East Germany, and Hungary in the 1980s. The increased religious activity was clear evidence that the officially atheistic communist regimes were not meeting the spiritual needs of many people. Most important, in the long run, was the Solidarity rebellion that began in Poland in 1980. Originally, Solidarity was a trade union movement, led by Lech Walesa, that campaigned for higher wages and lower food prices. It gradually became a nonviolent revolt against the entire communist system in Poland. The Polish government declared martial law in 1981 and drove Solidarity underground, but Solidarity leaders, aided by popular support and the Catholic church, continued to oppose and criticize communism.

1989

By the late 1980s several interrelated developments created preconditions for a major transformation in the Eastern European nations. One was the example of Solidarity, which sustained its opposition to Soviet communism throughout the period. A second was Mikhail Gorbachev's policy of *glasnost*, which encouraged open debate in the Eastern European nations as well as in the Soviet Union. Third was Gorbachev's realization that Soviet military commitments had to be cut back in order to save money for economic reform in the Soviet Union. The Soviet leader therefore let it be known that Soviet troops would no longer be used to repress rebellions in Eastern

European countries. Finally, these factors undermined the confidence of the communist ruling elite throughout Eastern Europe.

By late 1988 a series of strikes by Solidarity gravely weakened the Polish communist government. In an attempt to appease Solidarity the government agreed to hold an election in June 1989, and the result was a striking victory for Solidarity candidates. A noncommunist government was formed in late summer of 1989, and late in 1990 Lech Walesa was elected president of Poland.

In Hungary revolution was initiated by the June 1989 commemoration of the death of Imre Nagy, the reformist communist who led the Hungarian revolution of 1956 against Soviet domination and was executed that same year. The commemoration was such an emotional occasion that it sparked antigovernment demonstrations, and by October 1989 an unnerved communist government accepted a new Hungarian constitution. Free elections in the spring of 1990 led to the installation of a noncommunist government in Hungary.

The revolution in Hungary directly affected East Germany, for by the summer of 1989 the Hungarians began to allow East German refugees to use Hungary as an escape route to Western Europe. The refugee exodus incited massive antigovernment demonstrations within East Germany, sometimes led by churchmen and even by an orchestra conductor, Kurt Masur. East German rulers quickly lost confidence in their ability to rule, and on November 9, 1989, crowds of people broke through the Berlin Wall. It quickly became obvious that many East Germans wanted reunification with West Germany, and the East German government soon became completely ineffective because it lacked popular support. After a year of negotiations a reunited Germany was established on October 3, 1990.

In Czechoslovakia, antigovernment demonstrations, often led by university students, broke out in the autumn of 1989, and an anticommunist organization known as Civic Forum began to pressure the government for change. The Forum was composed mostly of intellectuals and led by the playwright, Václav Havel. A general strike in November convinced communist rulers to allow some noncommunist representatives into the government, and then, in late December, Havel was elected president of Czechoslovakia. Elections in June 1990 produced a government led by Civic Forum representatives, but disputes soon began to emerge between Czechs and Slovaks, the two major ethnic groups in the country. One source of friction was the fact that the Czech part of the country was wealthier and more advanced economically than the Slovak area. The disputes gradually became so serious that on January 1, 1993, Czechoslovakia was peacefully split into two new countries—the Czech Republic and Slovakia.

These influences quickly spread to Bulgaria. By late 1989 street demonstrations and a growing prodemocracy movement frightened the Bulgarian communist rulers, who soon lost control of the country. Elections in mid-1990 gave power to a reformed Marxist party, but street protests continued, and a new constitution in 1991 was designed to stabilize the political situation. However, in Bulgaria, unlike most other Eastern European nations, Marxist groups still exercised considerable influence.

The last, and most violent, revolution occurred in Romania, which had been tightly controlled since the mid-1960s by Nicolae Ceauşescu, a despot capable of great cruelty. A popular uprising against Ceauşescu in the last two weeks of 1989 became a virtual civil war in which many were killed. Ceauşescu and his wife were executed on Christmas Day, 1989. The uprising failed to produce lasting political change, however, because Ceauşescu's followers used the turmoil to reinstate control over the country. These followers no longer called themselves communists, but Romania remained a dictatorship with a strong secret police apparatus.

Thus, five of six Eastern European nations experienced relatively peaceful revolutions in 1989–1990. There was some violence, but, with the exception of Romania, few people were killed. Once Soviet support was withdrawn, most of the communist governments disappeared quickly, because they had little indigenous support. Throughout the 1970s and 1980s Eastern European philosophers, poets, and other intellectuals—such as Václav Havel in Czechoslovakia—had constantly criticized the tyranny of the communist regimes and thereby gradually undermined their legitimacy. That criticism, added to the economic grievances of the great majority of Eastern European peoples, destroyed whatever popular support communism had.[25] (For a discussion of the Eastern European nations in the 1990s, see Chapter 2.)

One other Eastern European communist nation, Yugoslavia, endured massive violence and warfare. The country of Yugoslavia was created after World War I out of the ruins of the old Hapsburg Empire. It was populated primarily by six peoples (Serbs, Croats, Slovenes, Macedonians, Montenegrins, and Bosnians) who were divided among three different religious confessions (the Serbian Orthodox Church, the Roman Catholic Church, and the Muslim community mostly in Bosnia). During World War II these ethnic and religious differences erupted into open conflict as guerrilla

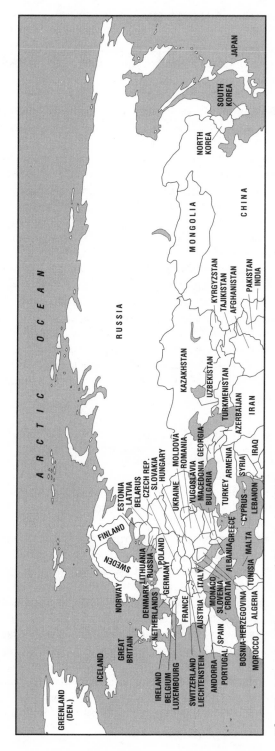

The New Europe: Europe and Russia in 1995

37

organizations representing different groups fought each other as well as the Germans, and a Nazi puppet state in Croatia sent Serbs and Jews, among others, to concentration camps. After 1945 Yugoslavia was dominated by the communist Josip Broz Tito, a national hero in World War II. He kept the country free of Soviet control, and his prestige and political skills encouraged cooperation among the various ethnic groups in Yugoslavia.

Tito's death in 1980 led to a power vacuum, as no one in the communist leadership proved capable of guiding a unified country. The authority of the central government gradually eroded in the 1980s, and different ethnic groups began to demand autonomy or independence. In 1991 the Yugoslav nation effectively broke up into five new countries—Croatia, Slovenia, Serbia-Montenegro, Macedonia, and Bosnia. War broke out almost immediately. Serbia, led by communist Slobodan Milosevic, who inflamed Serbian nationalism, fought Croatia in 1991 in an attempt to seize Serb-populated areas of Croatia. Then, in 1992, Serbia and to a lesser degree Croatia attacked Bosnia, as they sought to take control of Serb-populated and Croat-populated areas of Bosnia. The war in Bosnia was so savage that by 1994 over two hundred thousand people, mostly Muslim Bosnians, had been killed, and over two million were homeless refugees. It was the worst violence in Europe since World War II.

Why Did Communism Collapse?

The collapse of the communist system in the Soviet Union and the Eastern European countries was one of the most dramatic, most influential developments of the twentieth century. The collapse was caused in part by a failure of leadership and in part by a quiet rebellion in which ordinary people in the communist countries gradually stopped supporting the communist governments.

The fundamental cause of the failure of leadership was the Stalinist system itself, a system so bureaucratically rigid that it did not allow for peaceful change. The system encouraged people to follow orders and not take any initiatives. One result was economic stagnation, which gradually led to a decline in the quality of material life. For example, by the late 1960s the Soviet health care system was so ineffective that infant mortality rates began to rise, and life expectancy rates to decline. Another result was massive environmental degradation, as the Soviet system stressed industrial production and paid little attention to environmental problems. (For details, see the section "The Environmental Problem" in Chapter 2.) By the 1980s it was increasingly obvious to many ordinary citizens in the communist countries that the communist system was not working very well. Gorbachev believed that the system could be reformed, but he did not realize that the system had already lost much public support. When communism began to collapse in the late 1980s, Gorbachev was unwilling to resort to force to maintain himself in power, so in a sense he also repudiated the Stalinist system, based as it was on coercion and violence.

The quiet rebellion by ordinary people was a gradual process that began with the dissident movement—a small collection of artists, intellectuals, environmentalists, and some religious groups—that maintained a moral opposition to the tyranny and brutality of the communist regimes. Détente encouraged dissidence, and small human rights groups appeared in the 1970s. Gradually, growing numbers of people found ways to escape the control of communist authorities. For example, art institutes in Czechoslovakia began to hold competitions in which prizes were awarded by teachers and artists rather than by communist officials. Another example was books. Communist governments in some Eastern European countries allowed publication of such American novels as John Steinbeck's *Grapes of Wrath* and J. D. Salinger's *Catcher in the Rye,* on the assumption that the books revealed the decadence of American life; but ordinary readers often found such books to be expressions of freedom and creativity. By the 1980s many people had escaped spiritually and morally from the communist system, in the sense that they no longer took communist ideology seriously. The spiritual and moral escape was the foundation of the political escape—that is, the actual overthrow of the communist system.

There were, of course, many other causes of the collapse of communism. The costs of maintaining the arms race with the United States helped undermine the Soviet economy. The rebellions of various nationalities helped cause the disintegration of the Soviet economy. In the final analysis, however, the most fundamental causes were the failure of leadership and the quiet rebellion by ordinary people.

AN EVALUATION OF THE COLD WAR

The Cold War lasted from 1945 until 1991. Several times during that period, the United States and the Soviet Union appeared to be close to a military confrontation, notable examples being the Berlin blockade crisis of 1948 and the Cuban missile crisis of 1962.

However, fear of nuclear war always impelled the two superpowers to find a way to avoid direct military conflict. In the final analysis, the Cold War was a period of sometimes frightening crises and of a very dangerous arms race, but it never became World War III. American historian John Lewis Gaddis argues that we should refer to 1945–1991 as the "long peace." He notes in particular that, in terms of relationships among the most powerful nations, the years after 1945 were much more stable and peaceful than were the three decades before 1945.[26]

However, the fact that the superpowers did not fight World War III does not mean that the world has been at peace since 1945. According to one count, since 1945 there have been at least eighty wars in the world, killing between fifteen million and thirty million people.[27] Some of those wars, such as the Korean War and the Vietnam War, were a part of the Cold War conflict. Others, such as the Iran-Iraq War of the 1980s, were basically unconnected to the Cold War but were more destructive because of the weapons proliferation engendered by the Cold War. Both the United States and the Soviet Union (and other nations as well) sold or gave increasingly sophisticated weaponry to their allies, and the result was a continued expansion of the amount of military firepower in the world. A recent example of such expansion is the attempt of North Korea to produce an atomic bomb in 1993–1994.

The Cold War also played a part in another deadly phenomenon of the twentieth century, the genocides in which states and/or armies murdered large numbers of people. One estimate is that between 1900 and the late 1980s over 150 million people were killed in mass murder campaigns in various countries.[28] Some mass murders were designed to kill alleged racial or ethnic enemies, examples being the destruction of Jews in Nazi Germany and the killing of Bosnians by Serbs in 1992–1994 (in the former Yugoslavia). Other murder campaigns were aimed at those who opposed, or were thought to oppose, the ruling ideology of a state, the most famous example being the murder of as many as twenty million people directed by Joseph Stalin in the Soviet Union of the 1930s. Still others were wartime atrocities in which victorious soldiers killed the weak and defenseless. Such atrocities occurred in World War II and in the Vietnam War, to give just two examples.

It may be years before historians develop a thorough evaluation of the Cold War years. At this point, the preceding paragraphs would indicate a mixed judgment. The Cold War years of 1945–1991 were more peaceful than the World War years of 1914–1945. Furthermore, the Cold War ended quietly with the collapse of an often-brutal totalitarian empire. On the other hand, the Cold War contributed to a continued increase in the amount of weaponry and military firepower in the world, and that legacy will be with us for some time.

A NEW ERA

The world is entering a new era in the 1990s. In the previous era— the World War years and the Cold War years—the dominant issues in international politics were the rivalries and conflicts among the most powerful nations. The new era appears to be focusing on more diverse issues and problems. Some of the most important are the following:

1. *Democratization.* In the late 1980s and early 1990s, a wave of democratization swept across the globe. The republics that seceded from the former Soviet Union and several countries in Eastern Europe elected new governments to replace communist regimes. South Africa began to dismantle the apartheid system, and in 1994 Nelson Mandela was elected the first black president of South Africa. Several other African countries developed more democratic political systems at the same time. Civilian, elected leadership replaced military regimes in Argentina, Brazil, and Chile. Palestinians in some parts of Israel gained some limited local autonomy (see Chapter 3). In China, the 1989 Tiananmen Square rebellion was unsuccessful but exposed popular discontent with the government. Not all these democratic movements succeeded or will succeed in the future, but these examples indicate that the ending of the Cold War and the collapse of communism helped undermine authoritarian governments and release democratic impulses.
2. *Ethnic conflict.* Another form of assertiveness from below is the increasingly militant expression of ethnic and religious affiliations. Some examples are the Serbian war against Bosnians in the former Yugoslavia, the split of Czechoslovakia into Czech and Slovak nations, the assertion of anti-Muslim Hindu fundamentalism in India, the increasing strength of the Islamic movement in several Arab countries, the Kurdish rebellion in Iraq, and the 1994 fighting between ethnic groups in Rwanda. Some ethnic and/or religious movements are relatively peaceful asser-

tions of cultural loyalty by people seeking a sense of belonging in a chaotic world. Others are more aggressive attempts to destroy ethnic or religious enemies.

3. *Local wars and weapons proliferation.* Dozens of local wars erupted around the globe in the 1980s and early 1990s. Some were ethnic conflicts such as the Serb-Bosnian-Croatian wars in the former Yugoslavia. Others were civil wars in which different groups fought for control of a state, as in Zaire and Afghanistan. Still others were wars between states, as in the Iran-Iraq War of the 1980s. Compared with World Wars I and II these local wars were small affairs, but they were often very destructive because of the large amounts of military firepower available to combatants. In addition to the array of conventional weapons in the world, some nations such as Iraq and North Korea continue to try to develop nuclear weapons. A number of nations—including Libya, Egypt, Syria, Iraq, Iran, India, Pakistan, Brazil, and Argentina—have recently acquired ballistic missiles capable of carrying conventional, nuclear, or chemical warheads. Many of the same nations also have offensive chemical weapons. In short, the sophisticated weaponry that only a handful of very powerful nations possessed in the 1950s and 1960s has gradually become available to more nations, and the result is that local wars can be and are more deadly and more destructive than ever before.

4. *Globalization.* Some forces in the world today emphasize global interrelationships and interdependence among peoples, in contrast to the localized loyalties of ethnic groups. Supranational corporations and international financial institutions have created a global economy beyond the bounds of national states (see Chapter 2). Global communications and information technology carry the same business information, international news, and rock music to many parts of the world. Environmental problems are increasingly global, or at least regional, in scope (see Chapter 2). Some democratizing social forces are organized on a transnational basis, examples being the Amnesty International organization that monitors human rights violations around the world and the hundreds of grass-roots environmental groups that lobbied the "Earth Summit" in Rio de Janeiro in 1992.

5. *The North-South split.* The economic gap is growing between the nations of the North (the wealthy nations lo-

cated primarily in the Northern Hemisphere) and many of the nations of the South (the poor countries located primarily in the Southern Hemisphere) (see Chapter 3). The problems and issues resulting from the gap are enormous. Can the poor nations achieve some economic development, and should the wealthy nations help them in that regard? If so, how? Can the global environment endure the pollution produced when and if many of the nations of the South industrialize their economies in the same way the nations of the North already have? Can the rich nations, the middle-income countries, and the poor nations learn to cooperate in such matters as international trade and the problems of the global environment? Can these nations manage humanely the growing attempts of people to migrate from the South to the North in search of a better life? These and many other problems will likely make the North-South split into a major international issue.

6. *Shifting power.* The nations that dominate world politics will change. In the early 1990s the United States, the only remaining superpower, is experiencing economic problems. The Soviet Union no longer exists. Japan and the European Union, led by Germany, may exert increasing influence in world affairs.

SUGGESTED READINGS

Daniel Yergin, *Shattered Peace: The Origins of the Cold War and the National Security State* (Boston: Houghton Mifflin, 1978), is an excellent study of the origins of the confrontation between the superpowers and of how this confrontation affected, and still affects, American political life. Martin J. Sherwin, *A World Destroyed: The Atomic Bomb and the Grand Alliance* (New York: Knopf, 1975), focuses on the impact of the atomic bomb on American diplomacy and the origins of the Cold War. American nuclear weapons policy after World War II is covered thoroughly and incisively by Michael Mandelbaum, *The Nuclear Question: The United States and Nuclear Weapons, 1946–1976* (Cambridge, Eng.: Cambridge Univ. Press, 1979). A superb history of the Soviet nuclear weapons program is David Holloway, *Stalin and the Bomb: The Soviet Union and Atomic Energy* (New York: Yale Univ. Press, 1995). For a good analysis of the international political system and American foreign policy through the late 1970s, see Stanley Hoffmann, *Primacy or World Order* (New York: McGraw-Hill, 1978). A solid study of Europe's position in international politics after World War II is A. W. DePorte, *Europe between the Superpowers: The Enduring Balance* (New Haven: Yale Univ. Press, 1979).

For Soviet foreign policy before the Gorbachev years, a good, thorough analysis is Adam B. Ulam, *Expansion and Coexistence: Soviet Foreign Policy, 1917–73*, 2d ed. (New York: Praeger, 1974).

Two important works about the nuclear arms race are Alva Myrdal, *The Game of Disarmament* (New York: Pantheon, 1976), and Robert Jungk, *The New Tyranny* (New York: Warner, 1979). Myrdal, who won the 1982 Nobel Peace Prize for her work toward disarmament, provides a wealth of information on arms control treaties and negotiations and argues that the superpowers never seriously tried to achieve disarmament. Jungk's book is a powerful polemic against nuclear energy in all forms.

Several good works on the Cold War published in the 1980s and 1990s include the following: John Lewis Gaddis, *The Long Peace: Inquiries into the History of the Cold War* (New York: Oxford Univ. Press, 1987); David Calleo, *Beyond American Hegemony: The Future of the Western Alliance* (New York: Basic, 1987); Max Hastings, *The Korean War* (New York: Simon & Schuster, 1987); Michael Maclear, *The Ten Thousand Day War: Vietnam, 1945–1975* (New York: St. Martin's, 1981); James A. Nathan (ed.), *The Cuban Missile Crisis Revisited* (New York: St. Martin's, 1993); and Timothy Garton Ash, *In Europe's Name: Germany and the Divided Continent* (New York: Random House, 1993), an excellent analysis of détente.

On the disintegration of the Soviet Union, see Geoffrey Hosking, *The Awakening of the Soviet Union* (Cambridge, Mass.: Harvard Univ. Press, 1990), and Mikhail Gorbachev, *Perestroika: New Thinking for Our Country and the World* (New York: Harper & Row, 1987), which is an explication of Gorbachev's reformist ideas. Timothy Garton Ash, *The Magic Lantern: The Revolution of '89 Witnessed in Warsaw, Budapest, Berlin, and Prague* (New York: Random House, 1990), and Gale Stokes, *The Walls Came Tumbling Down: The Collapse of Communism in Eastern Europe* (New York: Oxford Univ. Press, 1993), are good on the collapse of communism in the Eastern European nations.

Two solid works on the future of international politics are Donald M. Snow, *The Shape of the Future: The Post–Cold War World* (Armonk, N.Y.: M. E. Sharpe, 1991), and Kathleen C. Bailey, *Doomsday Weapons in the Hands of Many: The Arms Control Challenge of the '90s* (Urbana: Univ. of Illinois, 1991). A good collection of essays discussing the implications of the end of the Cold War is Michael Hogan (ed.), *The End of the Cold War* (Cambridge, Eng.: Cambridge Univ. Press, 1992).

NOTES

1. Martin J. Sherwin, *A World Destroyed: The Atomic Bomb and the Grand Alliance* (New York: Knopf, 1975), pp. 232, 234.
2. A. W. DePorte, *Europe between the Superpowers: The Enduring Balance* (New Haven: Yale Univ. Press, 1979), pp. 64, 76.

3. Harry S Truman, "Truman's Speech to Congress, March 12, 1947," in Norman A. Graebner, *Cold War Diplomacy: American Foreign Policy, 1945–1960* (Princeton: Van Nostrand, 1962), p. 151.

4. Adam B. Ulam, *Expansion and Coexistence: Soviet Foreign Policy, 1917–73*, 2d ed. (New York: Praeger, 1974), pp. 518–520.

5. William Manchester, *The Glory and the Dream: A Narrative History of America, 1932–1972* (New York: Bantam, 1974), p. 678.

6. Michael Mandelbaum, *The Nuclear Question: The United States and Nuclear Weapons, 1946–1976* (Cambridge, Eng.: Cambridge Univ. Press, 1979), pp. 64–65.

7. Ibid., p. 89.

8. Ibid., pp. 64–65, 89, 212.

9. Ibid., pp. 36–37.

10. Manchester, p. 576.

11. Basil Dmytryshyn, *U.S.S.R.: A Concise History* (New York: Scribner's, 1965), pp. 235–237.

12. Aleksandr I. Solzhenitsyn, *The Gulag Archipelago, 1918–1956*, Vols. I, II, trans. Thomas P. Whitney (New York: Harper & Row, 1973), pp. 81–92, 93, 595.

13. Daniel Yergin, *Shattered Peace: The Origins of the Cold War and the National Security State* (Boston: Houghton Mifflin, 1978), pp. 196–200.

14. Dwight D. Eisenhower, quoted in Manchester, p. 660.

15. Walter C. Langsam and Otis C. Mitchell, *The World Since 1919*, 8th ed. (New York: Macmillan, 1971), pp. 441–443.

16. Ulam, p. 678.

17. Langsam and Mitchell, p. 444.

18. Alva Myrdal, *The Game of Disarmament* (New York: Pantheon, 1976), pp. 93–95.

19. Ibid., pp. 168–169.

20. Mandelbaum, p. 192.

21. Myrdal, pp. 103–107.

22. Mandelbaum, p. 118.

23. "A System That Doesn't Work," *Newsweek*, April 12, 1982, pp. 36–44.

24. Geoffrey Hosking, *The Awakening of the Soviet Union* (Cambridge, Mass.: Harvard Univ. Press, 1990), pp. 3–4.

25. Timothy Garton Ash, *The Magic Lantern: The Revolution of '89 Witnessed in Warsaw, Budapest, Berlin, and Prague* (New York: Random House, 1990), p. 136.

26. John Lewis Gaddis, *The Long Peace: Inquiries into the History of the Cold War* (New York: Oxford Univ. Press, 1987), p. 245.

27. Patrick Brogan, *The Fighting Never Stopped: A Comprehensive Guide to World Conflict Since 1945* (New York: Vintage, 1990), p. vii.

28. R. J. Rummel, "Megamurders," *Society*, September–October 1992, vol. 29, no. 6, p. 48.

CHAPTER 2

The Wealthy Nations

INTRODUCTION

From the perspective of the average person, the greatest achievement in human history may well be the prosperity which most North Americans and western Europeans have enjoyed for the last three or four decades. The ultimate sources of this prosperity have deep roots in European history. Over a period of several hundred years, western Europeans developed modern science, a dynamic capitalistic economic system, an industrial revolution using new technologies, and the power to take natural resources from many parts of the world. These factors, and many others, gradually made twentieth-century industrial societies rich, so rich that the average person in today's industrial societies lives more comfortably than any king or queen who lived before our century.

To comprehend more fully the transformation wrought by prosperity, we must remember what daily life was like for most of human history. Before the nineteenth century between 80 and 95 percent of all the people in the world were peasants. Hunger and the threat of famine were their constant companions. When food was available, it was unappetizing and monotonous at best. In Europe most peasants ate the same meal every day: dry, dark bread and gruel.

There were also disease and plague, caused partly by ignorance of the need for good hygiene. Our ancestors were extraordinarily dirty; they were infected with lice, fleas, and other creatures. Even the wealthy lived in filth. In the Louvre, one of the great palaces of Europe and for centuries a home for the French royal family, toilet facilities were scarce. Visitors to the Louvre commonly relieved themselves at bends in the corridors. The outside walls of the palace were soiled by the contents of chamber pots, which the chambermaids threw out of the windows every morning.[1]

By contrast, many people in Western Europe, North America, and Japan have enjoyed unprecedented affluence since World War II. This chapter examines the history of the wealthy nations since World War II.

THE UNITED STATES AND THE WESTERN EUROPEAN NATIONS

The Postwar Era

When the current age of affluence began in 1945, the United States was the only major nation that was genuinely prosperous. Americans developed an enormous industrial economy during the war, and by 1945 they possessed roughly half the world's productive capacity. Compared with the rest of the world, the United States was already a wealthy nation.

In Europe the years immediately after the war were a time of great hardship. An observer who traveled in defeated Germany in 1946 reported:

> For the Germans that was the *schlechte Zeiten*, the terrible times, worse for many of them than the war itself . . . there was no fuel, little work, little food; but their obsessive craving was for cigarettes. The country was governed by a cigarette economy, so that anything could be bought for packets of fags [British slang for cigarettes]— cameras, food, binoculars, girls. . . . When we drove into Hamburg it seemed not a city but a group of camps among the ruins; the rubble was flat, there was no shape. . . .[2]

Elsewhere, the situation was little better. France and Great Britain, nominal victors, endured food and coal shortages. In Eastern Europe millions of refugees fled westward to escape the spreading power of the Soviet Union. Yet, in addition to the physical hardship, most Europeans felt demoralized. Not only had they just ended a long, bitter war, but they also had to confront the moral question of what had happened in the Nazi death camps. Over ten million people had been murdered in those camps; it was a stunning revelation of what "civilized" Europeans had done to one another.

Under the circumstances it was remarkable that political and economic recovery occurred as quickly as it did. In Western Europe most major nations had democratic political systems in which a capitalistic economy was combined with welfare state social reforms. Great Britain elected the Labour Party, a democratic socialist party, to govern from 1945 to 1951, but then a succession of conservative prime ministers who accepted welfare state reforms governed until Labour returned to power in the mid-1960s. The French elected a series of coalition governments, all of them conservative, until Charles de Gaulle became president in 1958 and installed a new constitution that provided for a stronger presidency than before. De Gaulle dominated France until 1969 and was succeeded by other conservative presidents until 1981, when the socialists finally won an election.

In West Germany, which had to build a democratic system to replace the infamous Nazi dictatorship, the conservative Konrad Adenauer was chancellor from 1949 to 1963. He was succeeded by other conservatives, until the Social Democrats, led by Willy Brandt, won power in 1969 and held it throughout the 1970s. Italy, which had been controlled by a fascist dictatorship from 1922 until nearly the end of the war, also had to form a new democratic system. The Christian Democratic party, led by Alcide de Gaspari from 1945 to 1953, dominated Italian politics until 1993, although the Communist party regularly won about one-third of the vote.

Most of the smaller Western European nations also had democratic governments. In Scandinavia the democratic socialist parties were the dominant force. The only significant exceptions were two dictatorships that were holdovers from the prewar period. In Spain, General Francisco Franco ruled; and Portugal was controlled by Antonio Salazar.

Political recovery was accompanied by economic recovery. One important factor in Western European economic recovery was American aid channeled through the Marshall Plan. Another was the growth of international economic cooperation among the major capitalist nations whose economies were interrelated through trade and a number of other factors. Most leaders of the Western nations remembered how a lack of cooperation had hindered efforts to end the Great Depression of the 1930s, and they were determined to work together so as to produce prosperity for all. International cooperation not only hastened the development of prosperity in Europe and Japan but also helped to sustain the economic growth which already existed in the United States and Canada. (See a later section of this chapter for a discussion of Japan, which played a major role in the economic cooperation efforts after World War II.)

The first step toward postwar economic cooperation occurred in 1944, when representatives from most of the countries fighting against Germany and Japan met at Bretton Woods, New Hampshire. The Bretton Woods Conference produced two institutions designed to foster financial and monetary cooperation. One was the International Bank for Reconstruction and Development, better known as the World Bank, which was supposed to provide loans to assist in the reconstruction of war-torn Europe and Japan. Since that function was actually carried out by the Marshall Plan and other institutions, the World Bank concentrated on providing loans for economic development in the underdeveloped countries. The other institution was the *I*nternational *M*onetary *F*und (IMF), which sought to encourage international trade by coordinating the exchange rates of currencies.*

The Soviet Union and other communist nations did not join the two institutions established at Bretton Woods, but the capitalist nations continued to work together. In 1948 they formed the *G*eneral *A*greement on *T*ariffs and *T*rade (GATT), an international agreement designed to lower trade barriers. GATT became the principal forum for international trade negotiations and had some success at lowering tariff rates among the Western nations. (In 1994 an international trade agreement stipulated that GATT would be replaced by a new World Trade Organization. See "The 1970s–1990s: A Global Economy" later in this chapter.) A more recent means of fostering cooperation is the economic summit meeting. Since 1975 leaders of seven major industrial nations—the United States, Canada, Japan, Great Britain, France, West Germany, and Italy—have met annually to deal with common economic problems.

All these organizations and efforts to cooperate helped to produce prosperity. West Germany experienced what was called an "economic miracle," recovering so rapidly from the war that, by the mid-1950s, many West Germans had a comfortable standard of living. France transformed its traditional economy of small shops and small farms into a modern economy emphasizing technology and big business. Skyscrapers appeared in old cities, and factories emerged in the countryside amidst old abbeys and castles. Italy also modernized its tradition-bound economy and enjoyed sus-

---

*The exchange rate establishes the value of one nation's currency in relation to that of another nation. A fixed exchange rate stabilizes currency values so that a government or businessperson will always know the price of imported or exported goods. The IMF maintained fixed exchange rates until 1971, after which exchange rates were allowed to float.

tained economic growth. Great Britain lagged behind; its economy grew more slowly because of chronic underinvestment in industry. Japan carried out an equivalent of the German "economic miracle," and by the mid-1950s the Japanese had one of the most rapidly growing economies in the world.

Sustained economic growth produced major changes in the way ordinary people lived. In just twenty years—from the mid-1950s to the mid-1970s—per capita income (adjusted to account for inflation) rose from $3,365 to $7,177 in France, from $4,151 to $8,371 in West Germany, from $1,423 to $6,017 in Japan, and from $5,593 to $8,715 in the United States.[3] Consumers began to enjoy new rewards—for example, refrigerators, washing machines, automobiles, television, air conditioning.

Some—the homeless, those without adequate job skills, some racial minorities—did not benefit from prosperity. And some entire areas—for instance, southern Italy, the Balkans, the Appalachian area of the United States—remained mired in poverty. The majority of people, however, were prosperous.

The European Union

By far the most innovative approach to international cooperation was carried out by the Western European nations, with the support and encouragement of the United States. The destruction caused by World War I and World War II was so severe that many political and economic leaders came to believe that the European nations must end their competition and learn to cooperate if they were to survive. The chief spokesman for this point of view was Jean Monnet, an international financial advisor from France. Monnet believed that cooperation in Europe would stimulate prosperity and lessen the threat of war, so he devoted much of his time and energy to lobbying for creation of a "European Community." For his efforts he eventually became known as the "Architect of United Europe." (In 1967, most of the organizations described in the next few paragraphs were merged into an umbrella organization called the "European Community," so this phrase is used to describe the entire movement for Western European cooperation until 1991. In that year the Maastricht Treaty, discussed below, launched a movement to transform the "Community" into a more united "Union.")

The European Community actually began in 1950 when the French Foreign Minister, Robert Schuman, proposed the pooling of the coal and steel industries of Western Europe. France, West Germany, Italy, Belgium, the Netherlands, and Luxembourg accepted his proposal, and in 1952 the European Coal and Steel Community (ECSC) went into operation. Henceforth, the six nations allowed free circulation among themselves of workers, capital, and goods in the coal and steel industries. Emboldened by the success of the ECSC, the same six nations tried to establish a European Defense Community (EDC), which would have led to creation of a European army and a European foreign policy. The EDC was turned down in 1954, largely because several nations, especially France and Italy, were not willing to give up their independent foreign policy and armed forces. Nevertheless, the movement for cooperation among European countries continued.

A few years later, in 1957, the six nations formed a European Atomic Energy Community (Euratom) and a European Economic Community, or the Common Market. (The 1957 treaties were signed on the Capitoline Hill in Rome, a setting which symbolized the desire for unity in a Europe that had not been united in peace since the days of the Roman Empire. Hence, the agreement that founded the Common Market is often called the "Treaty of Rome.") Euratom was supposed to encourage cooperation in the research and development of nuclear energy, but for the most part it failed because the six nations continued to concentrate on their own national nuclear energy programs.

The Common Market, however, was a rousing success. The goal of the Common Market was to create one large economic market among the six nations by eliminating all tariffs and other trade barriers. Tariffs were gradually lowered until they were eliminated in 1968, and the result was a sustained economic boom throughout Western Europe. In fact, the Common Market was so successful that Great Britain, Denmark, and Ireland joined the organization in 1973; Greece joined in 1981, and Spain and Portugal did so in 1986.

The European Community was far more successful economically than politically, but the Europeans also established some significant political institutions. One is the Council of Europe, founded in 1949 to foster political unity among European nations. That unity has not been achieved, but the Council does serve as a useful debating forum for over twenty nations.

In 1955 the Council established a unique body—the European Court of Human Rights. The court is designed to hear cases involving violations of the European Convention on Human Rights. Over the years it has heard only a few cases, and it has no power to enforce its decisions, but the court has influenced public opinion and governmental opinion in the European countries.

Another interesting institution is the European Parliament, one of the institutions designed to hold the Common Market together. Although basically an advisory body, the Parliament has the right to approve the budget of the European Union. The Parliament originally consisted of representatives of the various governments, but since 1979 the members of the Parliament have been selected through direct election by the voters of member countries. Hence, the European Parliament is the world's first multinational legislative body elected by ordinary citizens and sitting by party rather than by nation.

In 1987 the European Community approved the Single European Act, which stipulated that all barriers to trade, not just tariffs, would be removed by the end of 1992. In practice, this means that business enterprises, capital, and workers are free to operate in any of the twelve nations of the Community. For example, a German worker can seek employment in France, Italy, or any other Community nation. As the Single European Act is gradually implemented, the result will be a very large free-trade zone in western Europe.

In 1991 the members of the European Community signed the Maastricht Treaty on European Union, designed to begin formation of a unified European federal state. In particular, Maastricht envisions European monetary union through a central European bank and a European currency. It also envisions development of a common European foreign policy on some issues, as distinct from the national foreign policies traditionally established by each country. The ultimate goal is both to increase European prosperity and to enhance European political power in the world. The Maastricht Treaty began to be implemented on November 1, 1993, after a long ratification process, so the goals of Maastricht may become reality over the next few years. However, the ratification process revealed that many Europeans in several countries (notably Italy and Great Britain) were uneasy and skeptical about European Union. They feared losing national sovereignty and national culture to a centralized, bureaucratic European state.

Nevertheless, the economic prosperity of the Union entices other nations to join. Austria, Sweden, and Finland were invited to join the Union in 1995, but Norway rejected Union membership. A major issue in the mid-1990s is the relationship between the European Union and the nations in the eastern half of Europe, now free of Soviet control. Some of these nations would like to join the

Union, but since their economies are less developed, they would have to be subsidized by the wealthier members of the Union.

The Welfare State

Another innovation of the postwar era was the creation of the "welfare state," a network of social reforms designed to ensure that all, or at least most, citizens of democratic societies enjoyed the benefits of affluence. A few social welfare programs had evolved in the past. In the 1880s Germany developed a program to insure some workers against accident or illness, and small unemployment relief programs were constructed in some countries in the first decade of the twentieth century. It was not until after World War II, however, that a complete welfare state developed.

The essential idea of the welfare state is that government should provide social insurance against old age and disability, access to medical care, economic benefits for the poverty-stricken, expansion of educational opportunity, and worker participation in managing industries. Not all these measures were adopted in every country—worker participation in managing industry never became popular in the United States—but the broad framework of the welfare state program was accepted almost everywhere in Western Europe, North America, and Japan.[4]

The first major nation to implement the welfare state program was Great Britain, where the Labour government of 1945–1951, led by Prime Minister Clement Attlee, worked to improve the living conditions of British citizens. Before 1945 British workers, like those in most countries, had little access to either medical care or education at the high school level and beyond and often suffered unemployment during economic depressions.

To alleviate these problems, the Labour government enacted major social reforms, including expansion of the nation's educational facilities, institution of a system providing virtually free medical care for everyone, and establishment of a broad plan of unemployment insurance. In addition, Labour brought the coal mining, steel, and railroad industries, among others, under state ownership, on the assumption that state control would ensure that these industries worked for the welfare of all citizens.

By the 1950s most of the other democratic nations established their own social insurance plans to provide funds for the ill or disabled and to guarantee a minimal standard of living for the elderly. (Some social insurance plans had existed before, but neither the number of beneficiaries nor the amount of benefits had been nearly as large as in the plans established after World War II.) New programs provided other forms of help. In France families received financial support to care for their children. Virtually all the democratic governments gave financial support to housing construction programs; and government control of industry increased, particularly in Western Europe. All these measures redistributed income in one way or another.

In addition to redistributing income, most of the democratic nations sought to expand access to education. Before World War II education beyond the elementary level had been limited to a relatively small number of people in most countries. Since higher education was usually a prerequisite for the most lucrative and powerful occupations, the effect was to reserve the best positions for the wealthy classes. Not only were the poor prevented from improving their economic status, but they were also denied the kind of education that would enable them to participate fully in the political life of their countries.

After 1945 the situation gradually changed, as educational facilities expanded dramatically. The number of British universities increased to fifty-two by the mid-1960s, and in France and West Germany university enrollment tripled between 1950 and 1965.[5] Most students in the European universities continued to come from the upper and middle classes, but educational opportunity was expanding. More people were able both to improve their employment prospects and to enjoy the intellectual and spiritual stimulation the best universities have to offer.

Worker participation in the governing of industry was implemented primarily in Western Europe. In West Germany a legal process known as *codetermination* established the right of workers to have representatives on the supervisory boards of most major industries. This right turned out to be relatively insignificant, because the supervisory boards meet infrequently. Furthermore, workers rarely have the technical knowledge or expertise to participate fully in major decisions.

Much more important were the "works councils," which were made legally obligatory in many Western European industries. These councils were, and still are, controlled directly by the workers and have certain powers, which vary in different countries and different industries. In some places the councils can demand important information from management; and they also have veto, or decision-making rights, in some areas. These powers afford the workers an opportunity to ensure that their work occurs in a safe, secure, reasonably pleasant environment.

By the 1980s the welfare state was an integral part of the political and social fabric of most of the democratic societies. As a result, these societies had changed dramatically. They became both more democratic and more stable. They became more democratic because the lower classes enjoyed a better standard of living, greater educational opportunity, and greater social mobility.[6] They became more stable because welfare state programs provided a cushion to carry people through hard economic times and ameliorated social and political discontent. In effect, then, the formation of the welfare state constituted a peaceful social revolution.

In the 1980s and 1990s, however, the costs of many welfare state programs increased dramatically. Growing numbers of retirees collected pensions, health care expenditures climbed, single-parent families needing government aid increased in some countries, and large numbers of people sought to enhance their employment skills by attending colleges and universities. These and many other non–welfare state factors helped create chronic government budget deficits in many of the democratic nations. As a result, public support for the welfare state idea weakened in some countries. In the 1980s U.S. President Ronald Reagan and British Prime Minister Margaret Thatcher cut welfare state funding in their countries, but in the 1990s the welfare state continued to be a significant component of all the democratic societies.

JAPAN AND CANADA

Japan

Japan is unique today because it is the only major industrialized nation whose cultural background is not rooted in Western civilization (the civilization that includes Europe and North America). It is also unique in that since 1945 a growing Japanese population has enjoyed a steadily rising standard of living, even though Japan has relatively few natural resources and a limited agricultural base. The shortage of natural resources means that Japan must import large amounts of food and raw materials and export manufactured goods to pay for the imports.

Japan began to industrialize in the late nineteenth century, when Japanese leaders realized that only a strong Japan could compete with the military and economic power of the European nations and the United States. The crucial event was the Meiji Restoration of 1868. The initial purpose of the Restoration was to designate a new emperor to replace a recently deceased ruler, but the more important result was to bring to power all the groups favoring the modernization of Japan. During the next few decades, these groups developed a new legal and administrative system to strengthen the power of Japan's central government, reorganized and modernized the armed forces, built railroads and telegraph lines to facilitate transportation and communication, imported foreign technicians and machinery, and encouraged industrial development. By the beginning of the twentieth century Japan had developed some industrialization, and by the 1930s it was strong enough to begin conquering an empire in the Pacific area. The United States and others resisted Japan's imperial ambitions, and the result was World War II in the Pacific. The Americans finally defeated the Japanese in 1945, the last blows being the dropping of U.S. atomic bombs on the Japanese cities of Hiroshima and Nagasaki.

American and other forces, commanded by American General

Workers assemble car bodies on a string of independent dollies at Nissan Motor's Kyushu assembly plant in Kanda Machi, southern Japan.

SOURCE: David Thurber/AP/Wide World Photos.

Douglas MacArthur, occupied Japan until 1952, when a final peace treaty was concluded. The Americans perceived Japan as a potential bulwark against the spread of communism in Asia and so supported a quick political and economic recovery by the Japanese. Politically, the Japanese developed, with American support, a new parliamentary system, more democratic than anything Japan had known before. By the mid-1950s the dominant political party was the Liberal Democrats, a loose grouping of moderates and conservatives that controlled Japanese politics until 1993. In that year an opposition coalition finally won control of the government and ended four decades of one-party dominance, largely because many Liberal Democratic politicians were implicated in a series of bribery and campaign financing scandals.

Economically, the Japanese began a rapid program of industrial development. The Japanese economy is characterized by close cooperation between government and business. The government Ministry of International Trade and Industry (MITI) sets production goals for certain industries, encourages acquisition of new technologies, and directs the general pattern of economic development. During the 1950s and 1960s the Japanese concentrated on production in heavy industries such as textiles, steel, and automobiles. High-quality products—Toyota and Honda automobiles, Sony television sets, Canon cameras—were sold all over the world. By the 1970s and 1980s, emphasis began to shift toward knowledge and information industries, and Japan became a major producer of computers.

By the 1990s Japan was one of the richest nations in the world, with the world's second-largest industrial economy and an average GNP per person of over $26,000. There were problems, however. One was that rapid industrialization produced severe overcrowding in many cities and major air pollution problems. Another was that Japanese exports were so numerous that by the 1980s Japan had large trade surpluses with a number of nations. The United States in particular accused the Japanese of unfairly restricting imports of goods into Japan and thereby creating major trade imbalances that threatened to undermine world economic prosperity. The Japanese response was that Japan lacked natural resources and therefore had to export to survive.

Despite the quarrels over trade surpluses, the Japanese and American economies became increasingly intertwined in the 1980s and 1990s. Japanese investors built factories and purchased hotels and real estate in the United States. Americans conducted an increasing amount of business in Japan and other parts of East Asia. In fact, East Asia led by Japan was one of the most economically dynamic areas in the world. The newly industrializing countries—South Korea, Taiwan, Hong Kong, and Singapore—were becoming steadily more prosperous and were major producers in fields such as textiles. Also, the Chinese industrialized rapidly in the 1980s (see Chapter 3). East Asia in the 1990s seemed poised to become a huge economic force in the twenty-first century.

Canada

Canada is one of the most prosperous industrial nations, with a GNP per capita of over $20,000 in the early 1990s, but its small population (approximately twenty-seven million in the early 1990s) leaves it overshadowed by its more populous neighbor, the United States. Canada and the United States often work together harmoniously on economic trade and many other matters, and trade will likely increase with the implementation of NAFTA (the North American Free Trade Agreement among Canada, the United States, and Mexico) beginning in 1994. One of the few areas of strong dispute is the acid rain from the United States that falls in Canada.

An ongoing issue for Canadians involves political and social cleavages. Provincial cleavages are strong, as Canada is so large that citizens often feel stronger loyalty to local provincial governments than to a distant central government. Most assertive is the province of Quebec, where large numbers of French-speaking Canadians threaten to seek autonomy or even independence from English-speaking Canadians.

POPULAR CULTURE

The term *popular culture* refers to forms of behavior and leisure activities that have wide appeal and are enjoyed by large numbers of people. It includes such public arts as television, film, and popular music as well as such activities as sports and shopping. Popular culture became especially prominent in the wealthy nations since World War II, because growing prosperity gave more people the time and resources to enjoy leisure activities and because television communicated popular culture to greater numbers of people.

This discussion of popular culture focuses on four elements of contemporary life: television and videoculture, rock music and "world music," sports, and the so-called Americanization of world popular culture.

Videoculture refers to the growing emphasis on communication through pictures and oral presentations rather than through writing, or print culture.[7] The most prominent element of videoculture is television. When commercial television first emerged in the 1950s in the United States and some Western European countries, television programming included news presentations, comedy shows, sporting events, soap operas, and a few dramatic performances. In the 1980s, as cable television created more channels, viewers gained more options such as rock music videos, classic films, and soft-core sex videos. Furthermore, businesses use television to advertise their products; politicians use it to sell themselves during election campaigns; and evangelists use it to sell religion. Much of this videoculture spread around the world during the last three decades. Soap operas became very popular in many countries, such as India and Egypt. Televised soccer matches attract large audiences in Europe and much of Latin America. American detective shows often appear on Chinese television. Watching television is probably the most popular form of entertainment in the world today, and in many countries the government controls television programming because political leaders want to influence what people see and hear.

Rock music, or "rock 'n' roll" as it was first called, originated in the United States during the 1950s. It was a new musical form which drew inspiration from the African-American music known as "rhythm and blues" and from the rural "white" music known as "country." The first rock 'n' roll stars, such as Bill Haley, Laverne Baker, and Chuck Berry, presented music that was openly sensual and sexual and offered a sense of liberation from the routine, bureaucratic world in which many people lived and worked. The first audiences were largely composed of teenagers, many of whom wore blue jeans (worker's clothes) but had enough money to support the new alternative music.

In the mid-1950s Elvis Presley, the most prominent American singer, was made increasingly famous by his television appearances. (Elvis soon gave up rock 'n' roll and became a movie star and singer of middle-class ballads.) He and many others popularized rock 'n' roll in both the United States and Europe. By the 1960s rock 'n' roll was called "rock" and was identified with the playfulness and rebelliousness of the 1960s protest movements. When the Beatles, the most famous British rock group, came to the United States in the 1960s, they were asked: "What about the movement in Detroit to stamp out the Beatles?" They responded: "We're starting a movement to stamp out Detroit." On a more serious note, Bob Dylan's "The Times They Are A-Changin' " expressed the mood of many young people during the 1960s.[8] The Woodstock Festival of 1969 manifested that mood, as more than half a million people came to a farm near Woodstock in New York State to listen to the major musical groups of the era and to revel in sheer physical pleasure.

By the 1970s and 1980s rock of various kinds was a part of everyday life in North America and much of Europe. The most famous rock artists were often strongly influenced by commercial considerations and produced relatively bland music designed to appeal to large audiences. The rebellious side of rock did not disappear, however. Communist regimes in Eastern Europe and the white apartheid government in South Africa censored the lyrics of rock songs, because such lyrics could express attitudes and emotions that were unacceptable to the authorities (such as having fun rather than obeying the rules). In the United States, "rap" music worried many middle-class people, because it was associated with lyrics that appeared to encourage violence and sexual aggression. (Rap was another musical form derived from the African American experience, its roots being in field hollers and call-and-response patterns in work songs.)

"World music" refers to various mixtures of musics from different musical cultures. Examples include Latin jazz, a blend of American jazz and Afro-Latin rhythm, and mixtures of Caribbean reggae with Latin samba or various African styles. World music first appeared in the 1960s, when, for example, singers Miriam Makeba from Africa and Harry Belafonte from the Caribbean recorded together, and Indian sitarist Ravi Shankar made concert tours in the United States and Europe. By the 1980s world music was increasingly prominent. In 1981 a WOMAD (*W*orld *o*f *M*usic *a*nd *D*ance) festival in Bristol, England, combined musical groups from Egypt, Burundi, and Great Britain. In the mid-1980s Paul Simon, an American singer very popular in the 1960s, collaborated on recordings and in concerts with a South African group Ladysmith Black Mambazo and Senegalese pop star Youssou N'Dour. By the 1990s *world music* was a broad term covering a growing number of musicians who creatively combined a variety of different musical traditions.

Most modern organized sports originated in nineteenth-century Great Britain, when the British Empire stretched around the globe and carried British sporting rules everywhere. One result is that the distinctively British game of cricket is still played and passionately followed in such former colonial societies as Australia, India, Pakistan, and Jamaica. In the twentieth century soccer/football is the most popular sport in the world, both in terms of the number of people who play it and in terms of the number of fans who support soccer teams. The United States is somewhat distinctive, in that several American-developed games—American football, basketball, and baseball—are more popular in the United States than is soccer.

After 1945 a sports boom enveloped much of the world, as growing prosperity provided more money and leisure time for sports, and television increased the popularity of sporting events. Several themes characterize post-1945 sports:

1. International sports competitions expanded, the most prominent example being the Olympic Games (revived in 1896 and modeled after the original Olympics in ancient Greece). During the Cold War, international games were often perceived as tests of strength and skill between the United States and the Soviet Union.
2. The developing nations in Asia, Africa, and Latin America were relatively new participants in the international sports boom. As many of these nations attained independence after World War II (see Chapter 3), they often supported the development of national athletic teams and individual athletes as a means of encouraging national pride.
3. Within the industrialized nations, African Americans in the United States and women gradually won greater sporting opportunities than had previously been available. Women athletes, such as Billie Jean King in tennis, helped increase the popularity of women's sports. Jackie Robinson became the first African American to play major league baseball in 1947; professional basketball and American football integrated at about the same time, although most university athletic teams excluded African Americans until the 1960s.
4. Sports have become increasingly commercialized, as television companies pay large sums to televise sporting events. One result is that star athletes often become very wealthy from athletic salaries and advertising contracts. A few athletes become international celebrities, examples being the Brazilian soccer star Pelé in the 1960s and 1970s and the American basketball star Michael Jordan in the 1980s and 1990s. Another result of commercialization is the gradual disappearance of many local, traditional sports around the world; with some exceptions, such as sumo wrestling in Japan and camel riding in Saudi Arabia, local sports are giving way to standardized, institutionalized international sports.

Sports have enormous appeal in the contemporary world. They provide much of the entertainment, the drama, and the excitement for large numbers of people. For the athlete, "The essence of athletics is in doing something supremely well. Not for the fans. . . . Not for the sportswriters. . . . But rather for oneself, for the satisfaction and pride that come with performing at one's peak." For the spectators, "Sports arenas are the theatres for modern man. . . . As did ancient Greek drama, modern sporting events invite vicarious participation in conflict, tension, and resolution."[9]

Several of the phenomena discussed in previous paragraphs—television and rock music, for example—originated in the United States, and as they spread to other countries, many people began to note the "Americanization" of world popular culture. U.S. news presentations, films, and television programs are often seen in the major nations of the world. (One wonders what a peasant in a poor nation thinks about the United States after seeing an American television show.) U.S. purveyors of popular culture spread around the world. The Walt Disney Company built a Disneyland in Japan in the 1980s and a "Euro-Disney" near Paris, which opened in 1992. The Kentucky Fried Chicken fast-food company opened a five-hundred-seat outlet in the middle of Beijing, China. U.S. products are sold in many parts of the world. Coca-Cola and Colgate toothpaste, for example, are advertised on Chinese television. These and many other examples indicate that, to some degree, the world is being "Americanized."

A TIME OF SOCIAL CONFLICT

In the 1960s and 1970s the North American and Western European nations experienced a prolonged period of political and social conflict in which millions of ordinary people helped to effect fundamental social changes in their societies. Questions of social justice were debated, as African Americans and ethnic minorities in the United States and women all over the Western world argued that they had been denied social and economic equality. The problem of war and peace was forcefully raised by the massive student protests against the Vietnam War and by the various movements protesting against the nuclear arms race. The nature of industrial economies was criticized, as the counterculture of the 1960s rejected what it saw as the indulgent materialism of affluent societies, and the environmental movement argued that industrial economies were despoiling the natural world.

Why did this era of conflict occur? It happened partly because the democratic nations were strong and healthy enough to encourage the growth of higher education. Furthermore, the spread of mass communication (radio, television) enabled more people to study and discuss basic political issues. Economic prosperity allowed people the time to become actively involved in political and social movements.

Another reason was the so-called baby boom, especially in the United States, where an exceptionally large number of children were born in the late 1940s. Wartime disruptions had prevented many young people from starting their families until then, and by the late 1960s many of these children were attending college, making up a large college population numbering over seven million in 1970. Partly because of their numbers, these college students were influential in American society; and they supplied much of the force behind the protest movements of the 1960s.

Some protest movements had begun in the late 1950s: Participants in the Campaign for Nuclear Disarmament in Great Britain and student radicals in Japan had staged a number of demonstrations against the arms race. But it was in the United States that one of the most prolonged protest movements developed. This was the civil rights movement.

The Civil Rights Movement

African Americans had always been excluded from the mainstream of American life. The American Civil War ended slavery, but for the next hundred years African Americans* continued to be oppressed. Living primarily in the American South, they were often denied the right to vote, were segregated into inferior housing and inferior schools, and could expect only the most menial employment.

World War II induced a growing number of African Americans to protest against racial discrimination, the argument being that African Americans had fought against Nazi racism and so should not tolerate American racism any longer. Then in 1954 the United States Supreme Court declared in the *Brown v. Board of Education*

---

*For much of the twentieth century, African Americans were called "Negroes," but by the 1960s that word had so many connotations of cultural and racial inferiority that many civil rights leaders began to substitute the word *black*. Using slogans such as "Black power!" and "Black is beautiful!" many young African Americans consciously sought to instill pride and confidence in African Americans. By the 1990s, the term *African American* was replacing usage of the word *black*.

**Martin Luther King, Jr.,
and Malcolm X in 1964.
These civil rights leaders
from the 1960s advocated
different approaches to
the same problem.**

SOURCE: Bettmann.

of Topeka case that "separate educational facilities are inherently
unequal." In the southern United States, where racial segregation
was often prescribed by state law, massive resistance to the Supreme Court decision broke out immediately. It was to be more
than a decade before real integration of public schools began. Nevertheless, the Supreme Court ruling raised the hopes of African
Americans, and the civil rights movement began to contest the
segregation of housing, restaurants, and transportation facilities.

In 1955 a bus boycott initiated by an African American woman,
Rosa Parks, in Montgomery, Alabama, eventually led to integration
of the public transportation system there. Then, in 1960, four African American students in Greensboro, North Carolina, sparked the
"sit-in" movement by refusing to leave a lunch counter where they
were denied service. The next year, 1961, a number of African American and white opponents of segregation launched a "freedom ride"
on busses traveling through the southern United States to protest
racial discrimination in interstate transportation.

Most dramatic of all was the August 1963 March on Washington, in which over two hundred thousand people came to the American capital to demand racial equality. They and the rest of the nation heard Dr. Martin Luther King, Jr., the most prominent leader of the civil rights movement, deliver a famous speech in which he said: "I have a dream that one day this nation will rise up and live out the true meaning of its creed: 'We hold these truths to be self-evident, that all men are created equal.' "[10]

These actions and many others exposed the harsh reality of racial discrimination in the United States. Eventually the American government began to respond by enacting civil rights legislation. The Civil Rights Act of 1964 prohibited discrimination in places of public accommodation, such as hotels, restaurants, and other business establishments. The Civil Rights Act of 1965 gave the federal government the power to ensure that African Americans in the southern United States had the freedom to vote. A 1968 law prohibited discrimination in the sale and rental of housing.

Thus, by the late 1960s legalized racial discrimination in the American South had for the most part been abolished. But then another racial problem reared its head. During the twentieth century many African Americans had migrated to northern cities, where they confronted racial discrimination just as pervasive, if more subtle, than that in the South. Furthermore, they came to the cities just at the time that many unskilled labor jobs were being eliminated by automation. The result was that, in the North, unemployment among African Americans was much higher than among whites; African Americans who were employed made less money than whites; and most African Americans lived in ghettoes.

A major spokesman for northern African Americans was Malcolm X, who was assassinated by another African American in 1965. Before his death, he preached that whites would never voluntarily eliminate racial discrimination and that African Americans must assert themselves through economic and social power. However, his words could not assuage the resentment and frustration felt by many African Americans. The frustration erupted into a series of urban riots that occurred in Watts, a Los Angeles suburb, in 1965, New York and Chicago in 1966, Newark and Detroit in 1967, and many other cities as well.

The riots frightened many people, but they also focused attention on the economic problems of African Americans. For a time the government attempted to alleviate these problems with many economic and social programs. The government sought to encourage racial integration in schools by withdrawing federal funds from schools that did not integrate and by busing white students to black schools and black students to white ones. The government also adopted legislation that gave African Americans support in their struggle to acquire jobs and educational opportunities.

Over the years these measures and others allowed some African Americans to improve their social and economic position, and the African American middle class was gradually enlarged, but many black people experienced little real change in their lives. Furthermore, by the mid-1970s, a conservative reaction began to develop. Many white people became convinced that school busing programs and legislation giving "preferential" treatment to blacks were unfair to whites.

In the 1980s and 1990s many inner-city neighborhoods were areas of violence and hopelessness for African Americans. Unemployment rates were high, particularly for young African American males. Violent crime was rampant in some areas, as the unemployed turned to selling and buying drugs and sometimes killed competitors in the drug trade. Many African American children were born to unmarried teenage women dependent on government aid and reared in fatherless households. Those who lived in the inner cities were isolated from the mainstream of the educational and occupational systems and so constituted an estranged "underclass."[11]

By the 1990s the movement for liberation of African Americans had a record of mixed achievement. On the one hand, society became more tolerant and abolished legalized racial discrimination. The movement also led to increased job and educational opportunities for some African Americans. On the other hand, racism continues to exist in the United States, and full social and economic equality for all African Americans is still a dream.

Antibureaucratic, Antiwar Protests

The nonviolent methods (sit-ins, mass demonstrations, etc.) of the civil rights movement served as a model for other protest movements, in particular the rebellions that occurred on or around many university campuses throughout much of Western Europe and North America during the 1960s. These rebellions were never well organized or well defined, and they never included most college-aged people. Indeed, many students and older people opposed the rebellions.

Yet a large number of students did rebel, and their rebellion took two forms. One was a political protest aimed primarily at two sources of bureaucratic authority—universities and the American government. Universities were a target because many had become huge institutions and had little personal contact with the ordinary student. The American government was a target for American students because many of them regarded the Vietnam War as illegal and immoral and therefore objected to being conscripted to fight in Vietnam. The other form of rebellion was social, the so-called counterculture: A number of young people rejected traditional ways of living and chose to live in communes, because they felt that affluent societies were addicted to materialism and mindless consumerism.

One of the first major episodes in the student rebellions occurred in 1964, when a dramatic protest took place at the University of California at Berkeley. The university administration tried to close a traditional student gathering place where organizations solicited support for various political and social causes. To prevent the closing, the Free Speech Movement sprang up almost overnight. Students charged the administration with trying to limit expression of political opinion, gathered support from large numbers of students and professors, and eventually forced the university to suspend classes. The Berkeley rebellion eased only when the university agreed to many student demands.

Within a couple of years the Vietnam War had exacerbated tensions on college campuses all across the United States. Many students opposed the war and were outraged that universities engaged in war-related research. More and more campuses were disrupted by student war protests, which were often led by organizations like the Students for a Democratic Society (SDS), which was originally a national student movement that was loosely organized and very idealistic. It argued that students had to help change a world plagued by war, racism, bureaucracy, and exploitation of Third World peoples.

By the late 1960s student discontent spread to Europe and Japan. In 1967 demonstrations against the Vietnam War— organized by students and nonstudents—were held in London, Paris, Berlin, Rome, Oslo, Amsterdam, and Tokyo.

The universities became the target of the largest demonstrations. Many lacked adequate teaching facilities, and corrupt practices existed in some. In Italy, for example, professors often held two teaching positions and sold copies of their class lectures for personal profit. At large universities, such as the University of Rome and the University of Paris, classes were held in big lecture halls; examinations were given infrequently, many students received failing grades, and little personal contact existed between faculty and students. This impersonality was the cause of many student demonstrations, which occurred in 1967 at the Free University of Berlin, the University of Madrid, several Italian universities, and in Czechoslovakia, Yugoslavia, and Japan.

Student protests peaked in 1968. In Europe the most significant outburst occurred in May at the University of Paris. Students took over several university buildings, effectively stopped most classes, and engaged in rock-throwing clashes with police. The student revolt triggered a massive general strike by several million factory and office workers protesting an income-eroding inflation. These events almost precipitated a full-scale revolution against the French government, then headed by Charles de Gaulle. In the end a compromise was reached. Some reforms were introduced into the French university system, and the workers won some wage concessions from the government. Shortly thereafter, the student protest movement in Europe died out.

In the same year a major student uprising occurred at Columbia University in New York. The revolt was precipitated by the university's decision to construct a gymnasium on university property at the edge of Harlem, one of New York's poorest areas. Neighborhood residents and many students felt that the university was flaunting its wealth. At the height of this uprising, student demonstrators took over several university buildings and had to be removed by police.

The next year, 1969, saw the peak of the demonstrations against the Vietnam War. The largest demonstration occurred in Washington, D.C., where several hundred thousand people gathered from all over the country. Another demonstration against the war, sparked by the U.S. invasion of Cambodia, became especially violent when, in 1970, Ohio National Guardsmen killed four young people during a protest march at Kent State University. A few days after Kent State, two students were killed in a civil rights demonstration at Jackson State University in Mississippi. After 1970 the student protests began to die down, largely because the United States started to withdraw from Vietnam.

Another form of rebellion for many students and other young people in the 1960s was the counterculture rebellion. Young people rejected the traditional middle-class values of hard work and "respectability." They argued that middle-class society was materialistic and mechanized. The hippies,* as they were called, insisted that

---

*The term *hippie* was derived from the beat-generation word *hip*, which was derived from the word *hep* used by jazz enthusiasts in the 1930s. Both *hip* and *hep* described people who were disenchanted with middle-class society.

the meaning of life lay in immediate experience rather than in a carefully planned future. They often lived simply in communes scattered around Western Europe and the United States, where they experimented with drugs, wore flamboyant clothes or clothes made of natural fibers, and celebrated the values of love, beauty, and peace. The counterculture faded away in the 1970s as many of the participants grew older and less rebellious. While it lasted, it revived an old idea in Western civilization, that people should live a simple life close to nature.

By the end of the 1960s a number of other movements began. Some sought to improve the social and economic status of certain groups within Western societies, while others focused on a particular political or social issue.

In the United States the example of African Americans inspired other ethnic Americans to attempt to improve their positions in American society. Mexican Americans, who live primarily in the southwestern United States, began to call themselves "chicanos"* and to seek access to better education and economic opportunity. American Indians, who often referred to themselves as "native Americans," also appealed to the government for better schools and economic opportunities. Both groups gained some recognition for their causes, but by the 1990s their positions in American life had changed relatively little.

The Women's Movement

Of all the groups demanding social and economic equality, women were by far the largest. The women's movement often referred to women as an "oppressed minority," even though women were not an actual numerical minority but rather a minority in the sense that they rarely exercised significant political or economic power. Many occupations were traditionally closed to them, and where they could work, they were usually paid less than men and were rarely allowed to attain leadership positions.

Changes did occur, however. In most Western European countries the legal position of women began to improve after World War II. French and Italian women gained the right to vote immediately after the war, although in Spain and Portugal women had to wait until the 1970s before they could vote. (British and West German women had won the right to vote before World War II.) Full legal

---

*The term *chicano* was derived from the Mexican-Spanish word *mejicano*, which means "Mexican American."

equality for women was written into the French and West German constitutions. Legislation mandating equal pay for equal work was approved in Great Britain and West Germany. Several countries liberalized their abortion laws, giving women greater ability to plan their families and control their lives. A few women attained powerful political positions, the most notable examples being Margaret Thatcher, who was British prime minister from 1979 to 1990; Simone Weil, who was elected president of the European Parliament in 1979; Gro Harlem Brundtland, prime minister of Norway for four terms in the 1980s and 1990s; Mary Robinson, who was elected president of Ireland in 1990; and Edith Cresson, premier of France in 1991–1992. (Women also led some Asian and Latin American nations, examples being Indira Gandhi, prime minister of India from 1966 to 1977 and from 1980 to 1984; Benazir Bhutto, prime minister of Pakistan from 1988 to 1990 and from 1993–; Violeta Chamorro, president of Nicaragua from 1990–; Corazon Aquino, president of the Philippines from 1986 to 1992; Khaleda Zia, prime minister of Bangladesh from 1991–; and Chandrika Kumaratunga, elected prime minister of Sri Lanka in 1994.)

Strong women's movements emerged in the 1960s and 1970s in Italy, France, and several of the Scandinavian countries. Yet, the lives of most women changed very slowly. Most women continued to fill subordinate roles within their families and society. Those who sought employment often were hired for traditionally female occupations such as secretarial work and were paid less than men.

The women's movement was very active in the United States. Many women had taken jobs during World War II, and the proportion of women in the labor force continued to grow after the war. By the early 1960s over one-third of all adult women worked for pay, and by the end of the decade the majority of adult women held paying jobs.[12] But most worked at low-paying clerical and service jobs.

In the 1960s some women began to protest their condition. In *The Feminine Mystique,* a very influential book, Betty Friedan argued that American society had brainwashed women into preferring the roles of wife and mother over other roles available in the job market. In 1966 Friedan and others founded the National Organization for Women (NOW) to advance the feminist cause.

Some of the women's movement demands were accepted, at least in theory, by most Americans. The principle of equal pay for equal work seemed reasonable, and gradually better employment opportunities opened up for women. Two breakthroughs occurred in the early 1980s, when Sandra Day O'Connor became the first woman appointed to the U.S. Supreme Court and Sally Ride became the first female American astronaut to fly into outer space.

By the 1980s American women had more educational and employment opportunities than in earlier years. However, they were often overworked because they not only held jobs but also continued to be primarily responsible for home and child care. Furthermore, women often earned less than men for doing the same job, and single women with children were a rapidly growing poverty group.

In the 1990s abortion was the most divisive issue associated with the women's movement. Many people, men and women, argued that choices about abortion should be made primarily by the woman involved. Many others opposed this argument vehemently, believing that abortion is little different from murder and that governments should prohibit most, if not all, abortions. The abortion issue was very difficult, because it brought fundamental values into direct conflict. The value of respect for developing human life confronted the value of compassion for women who in some circumstances face a terrible moral dilemma in deciding whether or not to abort a pregnancy. Most of the democratic nations in

Pro-choice demonstrator Bonnie Berko of North Potomac, Maryland, holds her placard while anti-abortion demonstrators march toward Capitol Hill, January 23, 1995. Groups on both sides of the abortion issue marched in Washington to mark the twenty-second anniversary of the Supreme Court's *Roe* v. *Wade* decision legalizing abortion.

SOURCE: Mannie Garcia/AP/Wide World Photos.

North America and Western Europe allowed abortions in at least some instances. Spain and Italy, for example, allowed a right to abortion only in cases of rape, serious danger to the mother, or serious malformation of the fetus; other nations such as France and the United States had somewhat more liberal abortion laws.

The women's movement faced growing opposition from political conservatism in several countries in the 1980s and 1990s. American writer Susan Faludi argued in *Backlash: The Undeclared War against American Women* (1991) that both the mass media and many politicians were trying to hinder the progress of women's liberation. Somewhat in contrast, Elizabeth Fox-Genovese contended in *Feminism without Illusions: A Critique of Individualism* (1991) that the fundamental problem facing the women's movement in the 1990s was a faulty conception of individual rights. She said that the democratic societies had evolved a radically egoistic conception of individualism in which every person was thought to be entitled to do whatever he or she wanted and that the women's movement should help define a new, more socially conscious conception of individual rights.

The Effect of the Protest Movements

From one perspective the social movements that originated in the 1960s were at least partial failures. Student rebellions died out without having accomplished any major institutional changes. Civil rights and the women's movements continue, but neither has come close to achieving its goals. But from another perspective, these movements were strikingly successful. Major social reform measures—civil rights laws in the United States, legislation improving the status of women—were approved in many of the democratic societies and as a result the lives of many ordinary people improved.

Most significant were the basic changes in attitude, sensibility, and awareness.[13] Social movements encouraged citizen activism, popular intervention in politics that survived into the 1990s. The 1960s also witnessed the emergence of groups—women, African Americans, and other racial and ethnic minorities in the United States—that continue to insist on playing a prominent role in the political and social life of democratic nations. In the 1980s and 1990s many democratic nations were more conservative than in the 1960s, but it was a conservatism that had to accept many changes (such as more women pursuing professional careers) that occurred as a result of social movements.

THE ENVIRONMENTAL PROBLEM

The environmental movement was the most significant of all the movements that began in the 1960s, because it raised the question of whether large-scale industrialization—the basis of modern economies—could continue. The movement began slowly when the debate over nuclear fallout in the 1950s increased public awareness of the dangers of radioactive wastes (see Chapter 1). Then, in 1962, an American scientist named Rachel Carson published a dramatic book, *Silent Spring*, in which she showed that pesticides kill birds and fish and could poison human food supplies. After that, a number of books and articles informed the public about pollution. In Europe the Rhine River was discovered to be virtually an open sewer. The Mediterranean Sea was shown to be so polluted in certain places as to be dangerous to swimmers. Many of the ancient monuments of Western civilization—Gothic cathedrals, the Greek Parthenon— were crumbling because of the vibrations and exhaust fumes from automobile traffic. Many cities in Europe and North America, such as Los Angeles, were frequently blanketed with smog, a kind of air pollution caused primarily by automobile exhaust.

The environmental movement began to have political impact by the late 1960s. The U.S. Congress passed the National Environmental Policy Act in 1969, and shortly afterward the *E*nvironmental *P*rotection *A*gency (EPA) was established. In Western Europe a "green movement" sprang up to pressure governments to protect the environment. West German environmentalists formed a political party—the "Greens"—which had some success at advancing environmental concerns. Great Britain set up a Department of the Environment in 1970; France established a ministry to protect the environment in 1971; and, also in 1971, Belgium passed two stringent laws for protection of surface and groundwater from industrial wastes. In 1972 a conference in Stockholm set up a United Nations Environment Program to deal with environmental issues internationally. By 1982, 144 nations had established environmental protection agencies.

Major environmental problems continued to occur, however. In 1986 an accident at the Chernobyl nuclear plant in the Soviet Union resulted in hundreds of immediate deaths and thousands more over the next five years. Much of the nearby farmland was severely irradiated, and many babies born near Chernobyl after 1986 were small and weak, probably from radiation damage. In 1989 the oil tanker *Valdez* ran aground off the coast of Alaska and spilled nearly eleven million gallons of oil into Alaskan waters.

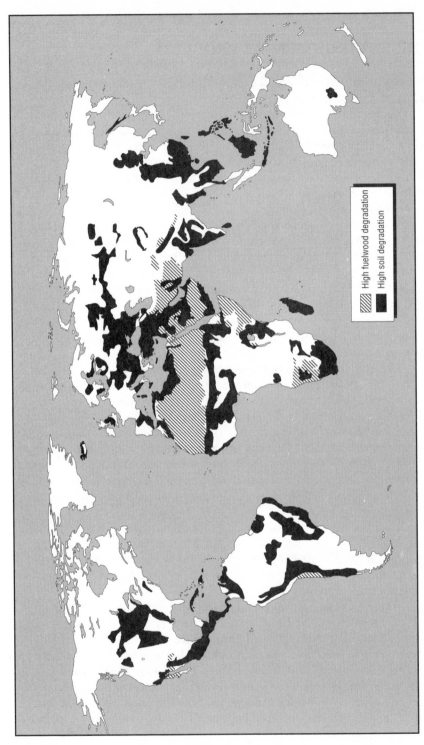

High human-induced soil degradation (*black areas*) is caused by water and wind erosion and use of chemicals. Overgrazing, overexploitation of vegetation, deforestation, and industrial use are just some of the causes. Areas where fuelwood resources have become acutely reduced (*hatched areas*) can support only a low population.

High fuelwood degradation

High soil degradation

Major oil spills occurred in the Persian Gulf during the Persian Gulf War of 1991. Major air pollution also resulted from that war, as Iraqi soldiers set more than six hundred Kuwaiti oil wells on fire.

The disintegration of the Soviet Union in 1991 was caused in part by severe environmental degradation. In fact, one historian says that the Soviet Union may have died by ecocide.[14] Most cities of the former Soviet Union were (and still are) heavily polluted, much of the farmland was overfertilized and under severe threat from wind and water erosion, and many rivers were choked with sewage. An extreme example was the Aral Sea, once the world's fourth-largest lake. The Soviet regime all but turned it into the "Aral Desert," as four-fifths of its water was diverted to irrigate cotton farms.

An underlying reason for all these environmental problems was the enormous expansion of world population and economic output after World War II. World population grew from 2.5 billion in 1950 to 5.5 billion in the mid-1990s; global economic output quintupled during the same period; roughly a third of the world's forests were cleared without replacing them; roughly a fifth of the world's topsoil was lost; and the ownership of cars and light trucks—major sources of pollution—rose from fifty million in 1950 to over four hundred million by the 1980s.[15] These factors, and many more, greatly increased the stress that humans place on the natural environment. Much of that stress emanated in the wealthy industrialized nations, which in the 1990s contained roughly 20 percent of the world's people but absorbed about 80 percent of the world's income.[16]

Of broad concern in the contemporary world are a number of problems that appear to be long-term threats to very large areas or even the entire planet. These include: (1) Acid rain, a form of pollution that results when air moisture combines with chemicals emitted by factories and automobiles, which is seriously affecting vegetation in eastern North America, central Europe, and southern Scandinavia. (2) Damage to the ozone layer, that part of the atmosphere that filters out much of the ultraviolet radiation from the sun, which is being depleted primarily by chemicals released from *chlorofluorocarbons* (CFCs) used as refrigerants and solvents. The long-term result of these problems could be increases in such human diseases as skin cancer as well as destruction of vegetation and crops. (3) Expanding industrialization, which has resulted in the buildup of carbon dioxide, nitrous oxide, and other gases in the atmosphere. Deforestation also contributes to the buildup, because vegetation absorbs carbon dioxide; the less vegetation there is, the more carbon dioxide is released into the atmosphere. The gas buildup is slowly producing what scientists call the "greenhouse effect," in which the gases act like a huge blanket that prevents heat from escaping the earth's atmosphere. The resulting warming of the earth is causing sea levels to rise (because of glacier-melting), and serious problems of coastal erosion and flooding of coastal cities could eventually occur.

A series of international conferences, many of them organized by the United Nations, attempted to address these problems in the late 1980s and early 1990s. In 1987 the World Commission on Environment and Development issued a report, *Our Common Future*, which called for "sustainable development," economic growth policies based on more gentle extraction of natural resources from the earth and more equitable distribution of these resources among the peoples of the earth. In June 1990 ninety-three nations signed the World Ozone Pact, according to which the production of chlorofluorocarbons, which deplete the ozone layer, will cease by the end of the twentieth century. The wealthy nations agreed to establish a fund to aid the poor nations in phasing out their use of CFCs. The Ozone Pact will not stop the depletion of the ozone layer anytime soon, however, since gases already released into the atmosphere will continue to destroy ozone for many years to come.

An attempt to deal with the greenhouse effect occurred at the November 1990 World Climate Conference in Geneva, when over 130 nations agreed to develop an international convention to combat global warming by reducing the amount of carbon dioxide released into the atmosphere. A major problem at the conference was that the United States, which is the largest creator of carbon dioxide pollution (primarily from automobiles and factories), was reluctant to commit to reducing that pollution.

In June 1992 a U.N. Conference on Environment and Development, popularly known as the "Rio Summit," met in Rio de Janeiro, Brazil. At the conference 154 nations signed a climate protection treaty, although the United States among others insisted that all specifics about reducing carbon dioxide emissions into the atmosphere be excluded from the treaty. In addition, 156 nations (but not the United States) signed a treaty to protect biological diversity. Perhaps more important, the Rio Summit began to define a new international agenda in which the goals of environmental protection and economic development of the poor nations were interconnected. The agenda recognized that the developing nations and the poor nations must pursue economic development (see Chapter 3) and that this development should occur in ways that protect the natural environment. It also stipulated that the wealthy nations should give increased economic aid to the developing and the poor nations in exchange for cooperation on environmental protection issues. Debate about whether and how to implement this new agenda will likely continue for years.

1970s–1990s: A GLOBAL ECONOMY

The world economy has changed significantly in recent decades. Some major characteristics of this change are the following: (1) The United States no longer dominates the world economy, as it did in the years after World War II. By the 1980s Japan and German-led Western Europe shared world economic leadership with the United States. (2) The economic growth rate of the wealthy nations slowed, compared with their growth in the period from 1945 to 1970. The slowdown was a symptom of economic problems, such as the loss of many well-paying manufacturing jobs. (3) A global economy has emerged, dominated by supranational corporations and financial institutions.

Economic Problems

The period from 1945 to about 1970 was an era of unprecedented prosperity for the democratic capitalist nations. But a recession began to develop in the United States around 1969, when government expenditures for the Vietnam War drove up the American inflation rate. In 1971 President Richard Nixon of the United States ended the Bretton Woods monetary system established in 1944 by refusing to allow dollars to be converted into gold because the United States was running constant trade deficits. The effect of Nixon's decision was to stop the practice of *fixed* exchange rates and allow currency values to fluctuate. (Since 1971 the democratic nations have tried to coordinate their monetary policies on an informal basis.)

The recession hit Western Europe in 1973 when the Yom Kippur War between Israel and Egypt led the *O*rganization of *P*etroleum *E*xporting *C*ountries (OPEC) to triple the price of a barrel of oil (see Chapter 3). Oil prices everywhere escalated. Since Western Europe was heavily dependent on imported oil, the price increases produced general price increases throughout the Western European economies.

The recession of the 1970s was characterized by high inflation, high unemployment, and a slump in productivity. In the democratic industrialized countries prices rose on the average of 7.7 percent in 1973, 13.2 percent in 1974, 9.3 percent in 1975, and continued to increase after that.[17] Along with the inflation rate came relatively high rates of unemployment, rising to over 10 percent in some countries. By 1975 there were seventeen million unemployed in the industrialized countries, and after 1975 the number got even greater.[18] The productivity slump is illustrated by a single set of figures: From 1963 to 1973 productivity in the industrialized countries rose by about 3.9 percent a year, but during the remainder of the 1970s the increase averaged only 1.7 percent a year.[19]

There were many underlying reasons for the recession of the 1970s. The productivity slump was caused in part by increases in raw material and energy prices and by declining investment. One cause of increased unemployment was that some newly industrializing countries (Brazil, South Korea, Taiwan, Mexico) with low-paid work forces were taking manufacturing jobs away from the traditional industrial powers. Another cause was that the industrial countries were moving from a manufacturing economy—which emphasizes steel, iron, and automobiles—to a high-technology economy—which stresses the creation and dissemination of information—and many workers in the older manufacturing industries found themselves without the skills needed for the new kind of work. A third cause was automation, as machines took over work traditionally done by humans. Ironically, the success of the welfare state also contributed to the recession. Old-age pensions and health care benefits enabled many people to live longer and thus collect more benefits. The costs of welfare state programs skyrocketed, leaving some governments with chronic budget deficits.

By the late 1970s some of the democratic nations began to recover from the economic jolts of the decade, but in 1979–1980 came another wave of oil price increases. That triggered another recession from 1980 to 1982. Recovery began in 1983 and lasted until about 1990. During this recovery most of the democratic nations enjoyed moderate levels of economic growth with low rates of inflation. Unemployment remained high, however. In the mid-1980s the Western European nations averaged between 9 and 10 percent unemployment, the United States between 6 and 7 percent, while the Japanese were able to keep their unemployment rate much lower.[20] Another problem was that federal budget deficits and foreign trade deficits were undermining the economic power of the United States. By the early 1990s the United States had the world's largest foreign debt, because it had to borrow so much to finance the deficits.

The economic problems of the 1970s and 1980s deeply affected millions of ordinary people in North America and Western Europe. Many endured chronic job insecurity, as large numbers of managerial and manufacturing positions slowly disappeared. Other employment opportunities were created to replace the losses, but many of the new jobs were low-paying, high-turnover positions in the consumer service industries (fast-food workers, hotel workers, and the like). As a result, many families needed two jobs to maintain a desired standard of living, and so particularly in the United States both husband and wife often worked outside the home. Even with two jobs, some families gradually lost the trappings of middle-class life, such as the ability to take vacations or to support university education for children.

Political Changes

Economic difficulties produced political changes. Political leaders in the 1980s and 1990s confronted problems resulting from chronic unemployment or underemployment. They often had to cut government funding for increasingly expensive welfare state programs. They periodically faced intense voter anger resulting from immigration problems. In Western Europe many voters feared that immigrants (from North Africa and other places) would fill jobs needed by natives. Anti-immigrant feelings were particularly strong in Germany, because large numbers of Eastern Europeans (from formerly communist countries) immigrated to Germany in search of a better life, and large numbers of refugees from the war in the former Yugoslavia sought safety in Germany. In the United States many whites feared job competition from African Americans or Mexican immigrants.

In the United States a conservative trend dominated national politics, partly because many Americans believed government taxes were too high and partly as a reaction to the social turmoil of the 1960s. Republican Ronald Reagan was president from 1981 to 1989 and was succeeded by George Bush, another Republican. In 1993 Democrat Bill Clinton became president. A conservative trend also existed in Great Britain, where Margaret Thatcher became prime minister in 1979, governed until 1990, and then was succeeded by another conservative, John Major. Conservatives prevailed in Germany as well; Helmut Kohl of the Christian Democratic party was the leading political figure throughout the 1980s and early 1990s and won another term in office in 1994.

In southern Europe the situation was different. Conservatives had been in power there throughout the 1960s and 1970s and so were held responsible when economic problems hit in the 1970s. The result was a turn to socialist governments. In France power passed to the socialists in 1981; the socialist François Mitterrand became president of France and remained in that office until 1995, when conservative Jacques Chirac was elected to the presidency. Spain and Portugal developed democratic governments for the first time in decades, after the deaths of the Portuguese dictator Antonio Salazar in 1970 and the Spanish dictator Francisco Franco in 1975. In both countries, reformist socialists were among those who governed from the late 1970s to the 1990s.

In Japan and Italy, corruption and bribery scandals involving leading politicians undermined traditionally dominant political parties. The conservative Liberal Democrats, who dominated Japanese politics from the 1950s on, lost their majority in the 1993 elections and were replaced by an unstable reformist coalition. Also in 1993 the Christian Democrats, who governed Italy from the late 1940s on, lost power to right-wing parties including some neofascists.

The New Global Economy

In April 1994 over one hundred countries signed a new *General Agreement on Tariffs and Trade*. GATT was created in 1947 to set rules for the international trading system (see the discussion earlier in this chapter). The 1994 accord cut tariffs on manufactured goods by an average of 37 percent. It also cut tariffs on some agricultural products and provided some international protection for intellectual property, such as patents and copyrights for books, films, and computer programs. To enforce the rules, the GATT organization will gradually be replaced by a new *World Trade Organization* (WTO), which was formally established on January 1, 1995.

The new GATT agreement is supposed to help govern the new global economy that gradually emerged in recent decades. In the 1990s the global economy was increasingly dominated by supranational corporations that evolved out of the older *multinational corporations* (MNCs), which were prominent from the 1950s through the 1970s. MNCs were companies owned by people in one country but operating in several other countries; they were usually identified with one country in terms of ownership and control. The new supranational corporations are characterized by multinational ownership (either by individuals or corporations), international management teams and work forces, and products made of components from several countries. (An example is the automotive industry, in which Japanese and American companies own considerable stock in each other's businesses.) In effect, supranationals are stateless corporations that operate beyond the limits or control of any government. Because they are stateless, it may be difficult to force supranationals to adhere to such things as environmental or worker safety regulations.[21]

The supranationals control an increasing amount of world economic output and world trade. Much of their economic activity is based on the technologies of the Third Industrial Revolution that emphasize knowledge development through computers and information processing through telecommunications (see Chapter 4). The supranationals thus tend to employ those who are well educated in high-technology fields.

The new global economy, based as it is on high technology, favors those people and nations who are talented, resourceful, and well educated, and it penalizes those who are not. (For example, a major reason for the disintegration of the Soviet Union was its inability to compete in high technology with other nations.) The world economy of the future may be a two-tiered economy: (1) A high-technology economy of supranational corporations would be based in urban regions that trade mostly with one another (such as New York, Toronto, Paris, London, Los Angeles, Singapore, Hong Kong, and Mexico City). These urban regions would be home to research universities, research laboratories, supranational corporations, and wealthy consumers who use low-paid, often immigrant labor to do unskilled work. (2) A poorer, less-advanced economy would include the poor nations as well as those people in the wealthy nations who do not or cannot participate in the high-technology economy. A two-tiered economy of this type began to develop in the 1980s. If that development continues, it will lead to greater wealth for some, but it will also widen the gap between the rich and the poor throughout the world.

THE NEW EUROPE

From 1914 to 1945 Europe was engulfed in violent conflict. From 1945 to 1989 Europe was starkly divided into an East and a West, into two hostile blocs of nations. In the 1990s, after the collapse of communism, Europe is in the midst of a fundamental political and cultural shift. No one knows the nature of the European future, but most Europeans hope that the old conflicts and divisions are giving way to a new era of cooperation and creativity.

One sign of a new era is new terminology. We can no longer speak of "Western Europe" and "Eastern Europe," as though they were two well-defined, monolithic blocs of nations. Rather, we must recognize the diversity in the new Europe. For purposes of this discussion, the European nations of the 1990s can be grouped in the following way: the European Union countries; Russia; Central Europe (Poland, Hungary, the Czech Republic, and Slovakia); the Balkan states (Bulgaria, Romania, and the states that were formerly part of Yugoslavia); and European areas that seceded from the former Soviet Union (Ukraine, Belarus, and the Baltic states of Latvia, Lithuania, and Estonia.) (See map on p. 37.)

The *European Union* (EU) countries are prosperous and democratically governed in the 1990s, and the Maastricht Treaty of 1991 is intended to increase European prosperity and power in the world. Prosperity and power create many issues and responsibilities. One is Germany. Germany is the dominant economic nation in the EU and will become more powerful if it succeeds in rebuilding the economy in the formerly communist eastern part of Germany (united with West Germany in 1991). An important question is whether the new Germany can use its economic muscle to assert political and cultural leadership of Europe. In short, can and should Germany replace the United States and the former Soviet Union as the dominant force in Europe? Another issue involves the relationship between the EU countries and nearby nations and peoples. The former communist states want and need economic assistance from the EU (and from others as well), if they are to have any hope of becoming stable, thriving societies. If they do not become stable, many people in those countries will seek to immigrate to EU countries in search of a better life. They will join the large numbers of Muslims who have emigrated in recent decades from North Africa and the Indian subcontinent. Some Europeans, particularly in the small neo-Nazi movements in Germany and France, resist the immigrant tide for racist reasons; others resist it because of fear that immigrants will take away jobs from natives of EU countries. The question is whether a democratic Europe can resolve immigration issues without unleashing the racist and cultural hatreds that afflicted Europe in the past and still continue in some places (Bosnia, for example).

Russia, once the heartland of world communism, is in the

1990s the scene of a dramatic attempt at political, social, and economic reform. Boris Yeltsin is president, the first democratically elected head of Russia in a thousand years. He governs in conjunction with a parliament that was democratically elected, which is also a rare phenomenon in Russian history. A fundamental problem facing the government is the transformation of a communist command economy that did not function well from the 1960s to the 1980s into some kind of prospering free market economy. No one knows with certainty how to do that. In 1992 the Russian government, following the counsel of American and western European economic advisers, tried economic shock therapy in which price controls were abolished and government subsidies of economic enterprises were removed. The result was that prices soared, production declined, and some members of parliament attempted an unsuccessful coup against Yeltsin in October 1993. In the mid-1990s Russia's economic reforms were not working very well. Many Russians were unemployed, and the crime rate was increasing. Many elderly were incredibly poor, because inflation destroyed the value of their pensions. Economic production continued to decline, in part because, with the disintegration of the Soviet Union, factories lost contact with many suppliers and customers, now in other countries. Some of the most talented Russians were emigrating to other countries, and some of Russia's most valuable resources—oil, gold—were being sold on the world market at extremely low prices so that the owners could get whatever money they could. Some Russians—those who imported foreign goods or exported Russia's raw materials—were prospering, but the reality was that Russia was in a major economic depression in the mid-1990s. Consequently, a growing number of people were disillusioned, fearful of economic change, and nostalgic for the old days when Russia was a world superpower. In the December 1993 parliamentary elections, neocommunists and conservative nationalists won more votes than the liberal reformers, indicating that many Russians were unhappy with the reforms attempted so far. The underlying problem confronting Yeltsin and other Russian leaders was that it is very difficult to transform a traditionally autocratic country into a democracy, particularly when the economy is severely depressed and most people's living standards are falling. Many observers feared that Russia would collapse into chaos; the hope was that the chaos would be a prelude to a more humane society than Russians had experienced under communism.

The Central European states contain some heavily industrial-

ized areas but also many poverty-stricken rural areas. In an effort
to develop a market capitalist system quickly, Poland, Hungary,
and to a lesser degree Czechoslovakia (before it split in 1993 into
the Czech Republic and Slovakia) resorted to economic shock therapy in 1990, just as Russia did in 1992. The results were the same
as in Russia, as high inflation and unemployment followed the
abolition of price controls and the removal of government subsidies of economic enterprises. By 1992–1993 a growing number of
people were nostalgic for the old days when communist regimes
guaranteed employment and kept food and housing costs low
through government subsidies. Also, economic fears led to attempts to identify scapegoats, and anti-Semitic and antiforeigner
movements appeared in some places. In 1993–1994 the shock therapy philosophy was moderated, and the Central European states
sought less drastic means of achieving economic change. Fortunately, the governments of these states were relatively stable. Lech
Walesa, the hero of the Solidarity resistance to Polish communism,
remained president of Poland. Václav Havel, leader of the Czech
resistance to communism, remained president of the Czech Republic. In Hungary, elections in 1994 returned the former communists,
now called socialists, to power, but they were thought to be reformist democrats who would carry out economic reforms. Slovakia,
recently separated from Czechoslovakia, was the most economically depressed country in Central Europe.

The Balkan states were for the most part poorer than the
Central European states under communism, and since the collapse
of communism they have accomplished less reform. As discussed
in Chapter 1, the states of the former Yugoslavia were engulfed in
warfare from 1991 on, and the results included mass human suffering and economic disruption. In Romania, which had the most
violent revolution in 1989, the former communists remained in
power under a new name, and the old secret police continued to
function. Still, Romanians had some of the trappings of democracy,
including a relatively free press. Bulgaria was also governed by
former communists, who claimed to be reformers. They have
privatized some state-controlled industries, but Bulgaria has remained economically depressed.

The European areas that seceded from the former Soviet
Union (Ukraine, Belarus, Latvia, Lithuania, Estonia) were technically a part of the CIS, the Commonwealth of Independent States
that on paper was a federation succeeding the Soviet Union. In
reality, these were independent states, each trying to build new
political and economic systems after the fall of communism. The

Baltic states—Latvia, Lithuania, Estonia—did relatively well economically in the early 1990s, partly because their geographical
proximity to the Scandinavian countries and Germany facilitated
commerce. In contrast, Ukraine and Belarus suffered severe economic hardship. Their factories, which once had received supplies
from the Soviet Union and had served customers in the Soviet
Union, were in the early 1990s cut off from Russia by national
boundaries. The effect was to encourage smuggling, corruption,
and crime, as some people sought and found illegal ways to make
money. Ukraine and Belarus had an additional problem, in that the
Chernobyl nuclear plant that exploded in 1986 is near the border of
the two countries (but in Ukraine). Much surrounding farmland
was contaminated with radioactivity, and thousands of people suffered from radiation sickness.

All the former communist countries faced very difficult political and economic problems in the mid-1990s. They also faced even
more difficult human problems. One was the lack of democratic
leadership, of political and economic leaders accustomed to working in an open society. The expert personnel were mostly former
communists trained to work in a command system, while those who
led the democratic revolutions against communism were ordinary
citizens inexperienced at guiding political institutions or economic
enterprises. Other problems arose from the habits and attitudes of
many ordinary people. Under the communist regimes people were
encouraged to obey orders and to let the authorities make decisions,
but in an open society people must learn how to take initiatives and
accept responsibility for their own decisions. A third concern was
the cynicism engendered under communism; the communist regimes paid lip service to great ideals such as economic equality and
justice, but their performance rarely even approximated the ideal.
The result was that many in the former communist countries became and remain deeply skeptical of all political programs and
ideals.[22]

In the opinion of many thoughtful people, a crisis of the human spirit also existed in the democratic societies of western Europe and North America. It is interesting to note the impression of
a German writer upon first coming to western Europe after leaving
communist East Germany in 1989: "The most disappointing thing
about the west is that there is no spiritual alternative here, only an
economic one—making a living in the broadest sense of the word,
but not making sense of one's life. . . . Getting ahead, eating, being
well-groomed—the lesser things of life have been cultivated to the
utmost and made into the higher things of life."[23]

The new Europe faces many problems but also has many opportunities. Perhaps most important is the possibility of rejuvenating the human spirit. (For a discussion of political and religious ideas, see the sections on "Democratic Thought" and "The Search for Meaning" in Chapter 4.)

SUGGESTED READINGS

Fernand Braudel is one of the most important historians of the twentieth century. His *Capitalism and Material Life, 1400–1800* (New York: Harper & Row, 1973) offers an excellent view of how ordinary people lived before the nineteenth century.

A good anecdotal survey of the 1960s social movements in the United States is Godfrey Hodgson, *America in Our Time* (Garden City, N.Y.: Doubleday, 1976). Also see Todd Gitlin, *The Sixties* (New York: Bantam, 1987), the memoir of one who participated in and defends the Sixties' movements; John Hope Franklin, *From Slavery to Freedom* (New York: Knopf, 1979), on the history of African Americans; Taylor Branch, *Parting the Waters: America in the King Years, 1954–63* (New York: Simon & Schuster, 1988), on the early years of the civil rights movement; and Malcolm X and Alex Haley, *The Autobiography of Malcolm X* (New York: Ballantine, 1973).

Gerard Piel, *Only One World: Our Own to Keep* (New York: W. H. Freeman, 1992), and Barry Commoner, *Making Peace with the Planet* (New York: Pantheon, 1990), offers good analysis of the environmental problem. For the women's movement, Lynne B. Iglitzin and Ruth Ross, eds., *Women in the World: A Comparative Study* (Santa Barbara, Calif.: Clio, 1976), offers a collection of essays on the status of women throughout the world, and Gisela Kaplan, *Contemporary Western European Feminism* (New York: NYU Press, 1992) is good on feminism in western Europe. On the European Union, see *Europe: Dream, Adventure, Reality* (Westport, Conn.: Greenwood, 1987), a collection of essays on the history and achievements of the Union.

For individual countries, see Frederick Siegel, *Troubled Journey: From Pearl Harbor to Ronald Reagan* (New York: Hill and Wang, 1984), on the United States; John Ardagh, *France in the 1980s* (New York: Penguin, 1982), on France; Henry A. Turner, Jr., *The Two Germanies since 1945: East and West* (New Haven: Yale Univ. Press, 1987), on the Germanies prior to reunification; Stanley Payne, *The Franco Regime, 1936–1975* (Madison: Univ. of Wisconsin, 1987), on Spain; and Edwin O. Reischauer, *The Japanese Today: Change and Continuity* (Cambridge, Mass.: Belknap Press of Harvard Univ. Press, 1988).

The journal *Current History* offers good analyses of contemporary events throughout the world.

NOTES

1. Fernand Braudel, *Capitalism and Material Life, 1400–1800*, trans. Miriam Kochan (New York: Harper & Row, 1973), pp. 437–438.

2. Anthony Sampson, *Anatomy of Europe* (New York: Harper & Row, 1968), p. vii.

3. A. W. DePorte, *Europe between the Superpowers: The Enduring Balance* (New Haven: Yale University Press, 1979), pp. 198–199.

4. Peter N. Stearns, *European Society in Upheaval: Social History since 1750*, 2d ed. (New York: Macmillan, 1975), pp. 302–303.

5. Robert O. Paxton, *Europe in the Twentieth Century* (New York: Harcourt Brace Jovanovich, 1975), pp. 577–578.

6. David E. Sumler, *A History of Europe in the Twentieth Century* (Homewood, Ill.: Dorsey, 1973), p. 409.

7. Marshall W. Fishwick, *Common Culture and the Great Tradition* (Westport, Conn.: Greenwood Press, 1982), p. 75.

8. Don J. Hibbard and Carol Kaleialoha, *The Role of Rock* (Englewood Cliffs, N.J.: Prentice-Hall, 1983), pp. 28, 79.

9. William J. Baker, *Sports in the Western World* (Totowa, N.J.: Rowman and Littlefield, 1982), pp. 337–338.

10. Dr. Martin Luther King, Jr., quoted in Godfrey Hodgson, *America in Our Time* (Garden City, N.Y.: Doubleday, 1976), p. 157.

11. William Julius Wilson, *The Truly Disadvantaged* (Chicago: Univ. of Chicago Press, 1987), p. 8.

12. Barbara Sinclair Deckard, *The Women's Movement: Political, Socioeconomic, and Psychological Issues* (New York: Harper & Row, 1975), p. 322.

13. Morris Dickstein, *Gates of Eden: American Culture in the Sixties* (New York: Basic, 1977), p. 27.

14. Murray Feshbach and Alfred Friendly, Jr. *Ecocide in the USSR: Health and Nature under Siege* (Basic Books, 1992), p. 1.

15. Peter Raven, "Defining Biodiversity," *Nature Conservancy*, January–February 1994, vol. 44, no. 1, p. 14.

16. Sandra Postel, "Carrying Capacity: Earth's Bottom Line," in Lester Brown et. al., *State of the World, 1994*, (New York: Norton, 1994), p. 5.

17. DePorte, pp. 210–211.

18. Jan Tinbergen (coordinator), *RIO: Reshaping the International Order* (New York: New American Library, 1977), p. 14.

19. World Bank, *World Development Report, 1980* (New York: Oxford Univ. Press, 1980), p. 5.

20. World Bank, *World Development Report, 1986* (New York: Oxford Univ. Press, 1986), pp. 1, 15.

21. Donald M. Snow, *The Shape of the Future: The Post–Cold War World* (Armonk, N.Y.: M. E. Sharpe, 1991), p. 56.

22. Erazim Kohák, "Ashes, Ashes . . . Central Europe after Forty Years," *Daedalus*, Spring 1992, vol. 121, no. 2, pp. 198–203.

23. Martin Ahrends, "In the Belly of the Beast," *World Press Review*, June 1991, pp. 21–22.

CHAPTER 3

The Developing Nations and the Poor Nations

INTRODUCTION

A fundamental fact of contemporary history is that the world is divided into wealthy nations and poor nations, that most nations in Asia, Africa, and Latin America are significantly poorer than the wealthy nations in North America, Europe, and Japan. Some "newly industrialized" countries and some "developing" countries (see below for an explanation of this terminology) have made some economic progress in recent decades, and in many of the poor countries small upper classes enjoy a comfortable standard of living. But most nations in Asia, Africa, and Latin America contain large numbers of people who are chronically malnourished, particularly susceptible to deadly diseases, and live in squalor.

The plight of the poor is deeply rooted in history. In many areas, a small upper class has for centuries owned most of the land, thus dominating agriculture, and controlled governments and political decisions. As a result, the lower classes had neither economic resources nor political power and were condemned to a life of poverty. This domination of the lower classes by the upper classes on a national scale has been, in recent centuries, exacerbated by the domination of the wealthy nations over the poor nations. From the seventeenth through the twentieth centuries, the nations of Asia, Africa, and Latin America increasingly sold low-priced agricultural products and mineral resources to Europeans and North Americans in exchange for high-priced manufactured goods. The result was the slow creation of a worldwide capitalist economy, in which the wealthy nations of Europe, North America, and, later, Japan got rich from the sale of manufactures, while the poor nations of Asia, Africa, and Latin America remained poor because they sold products that enriched the few (large landowners, for example) but left the many in poverty.

This chapter examines two major historical developments involving the poor nations. The first was a movement for national political freedom: Since World War II over one hundred countries have gained national independence. The second is a quest for economic development: The poor nations are seeking to overcome their poverty.

Chapter 3 is divided into two main sections. The first section summarizes some of the most important political developments since 1945. Four geographical areas are covered: Asia, the Muslim world, sub-Saharan Africa, and Latin America. Since it is impossible to consider in detail every country in these areas, only the most important developments will be mentioned. Four particularly significant subjects—China, the Arab-Israeli conflict, South Africa, and Mexico—will be studied in some detail. The second section examines the political, economic, social, and environmental problems afflicting the poor nations, as well as some of the proposals designed to try to resolve these problems.

The history of the poor nations since 1945 is intertwined with that of the wealthy nations. In the past, the wealthy nations controlled the empires from which the poor nations had to wrest their political independence. Today, the rich nations have the wealth and economic power that the poor nations would like to share. Several sets of terminology have evolved to describe the relationship between the wealthy nations and the poor nations. One used to designate the wealthy, capitalist nations as the "First World," the communist states of Europe as the "Second World," and the poor nations as the "Third World." This terminology is now somewhat outdated, since communism largely disappeared from Europe in the late 1980s and since some formerly Third World nations are no longer poor. But the First World–Third World terminology is still useful because it refers to a division between the powerful and the powerless. The First World nations dominate global politics and economics, while Third World nations have relatively little influence on world events.

Another set of terminology describes the world as divided between "North" and "South," since most of the wealthy nations are in the Northern Hemisphere, while most of the poor are in the Southern Hemisphere. Still another set of terminology uses the concept of "economic development" to describe groups of nations; the wealthy nations are "developed" (that is, industrialized and prosperous); the "newly industrialized" countries (such as Singapore, Taiwan, and South Korea) have recently become developed; the "developing" countries (such as Mexico, China, and Brazil) have large industrial sectors but also large percentages of poor people; and the "least developed" countries (such as Haiti, Ethiopia, and Bangladesh) remain overwhelmingly agricultural and poor.

A simple way of thinking about the world population in the mid-1990s is to envision it in the form of a pyramid. At the top is a small transnational political and economic elite, the wealthy and powerful from both the rich and the poor nations. Below them is a more or less permanently employed middle class of businesspeople and professionals. Many people in the wealthy nations are in this class. At the base of the pyramid are the vast numbers of the poor, including large numbers of people in Asia, Africa, and Latin America as well as some in the wealthy nations.[1]

DECOLONIZATION AND SUBSEQUENT POLITICAL DEVELOPMENTS

For the last several centuries, many of today's poor nations were colonies within European empires. Since 1945 these empires have virtually disappeared, as a wave of decolonization swept over the globe and most of the colonies gained political independence.* The scope of the decolonization movement is illustrated by the changes in the United Nations membership rolls. When the UN was founded in 1945, it had 51 charter members. Today the membership list counts approximately 180 members.

To some degree, the colonization process ultimately created the seeds of its own destruction. When the European nations conquered and ruled colonies during previous centuries, they undermined the traditional ways of life that had existed, and as a result the traditional rulers (for example, Indian sultans or African chiefs) began to lose their power. In their place came a new genera-

---

*Great Britain and France sought to retain a connection with their former colonies. Hence, the British "Commonwealth of Nations" is an association of independent states, mostly former British colonies, which are linked by a common acknowledgment of the British monarch as Commonwealth head. The members meet periodically to discuss political issues and exchange information. The "French Community," created by Charles de Gaulle in 1958, was designed to maintain a continuing relationship between France and its former colonies. As an organization the Community has almost disappeared, but France still has many cultural and economic agreements with its former colonies.

tion of leaders, men like Mohandas Gandhi in India and Kwame Nkrumah in Ghana, who were often Western-educated and sufficiently aggressive to challenge the power of the colonial rulers. This new generation was able to appeal to people and lead national independence movements.

Another way in which colonization could lead to decolonization was through the introduction of Christianity into colonial areas. Christian missionaries enthusiastically spread messages about "love" and the "brotherhood of man," even though these messages were incompatible with the racial discrimination and economic exploitation that were often a fundamental part of colonialism. Thus, Christian leaders unintentionally provided moral and spiritual support for demands that colonial domination be ended.[2]

The most direct cause of decolonization was the resistance of Asians and Africans to colonial rule. That resistance drove up the costs of empire at a time (after World War II) when most Europeans were unwilling to pay the taxes to maintain the military forces necessary to continue colonial empires. Furthermore, Allied propaganda during the war stressed the need for "freedom" and "liberation" of oppressed peoples from German and Japanese domination, and that propaganda encouraged colonial subjects to demand the same freedom and liberation for themselves.[3]

Asia

India   One of the first revolts against colonial rule arose in the Asian subcontinent of India. The main agent of Indian struggle for independence from the British Empire was the Indian National Congress, founded in 1885, though independence was not originally its goal. After World War I the Congress movement fell under the sway of Mohandas Gandhi, a devout Hindu who used nonviolent resistance in an effort to force the British out of India. Gandhi's nonviolent resistance—fasting in prison, nonviolent marches, boycotts, and demonstrations—was both a personal creed and a technique for preventing conflict between countries and communities. He drew his beliefs from Hinduism, the Sermon on the Mount, and the writings of Leo Tolstoy and Henry David Thoreau. His methods influenced, among others, the American civil rights leader, Martin Luther King, Jr., and Nelson Mandela of South Africa.

Gandhi was unique among twentieth-century revolutionary leaders because he was more a spiritual leader than a political leader. He became known throughout the world as a modern saint, and his Hindu followers bestowed on him the designation of "Mahatma," or "great soul." His efforts were so effective that in 1947 the British granted India independence. By then, religious differences between the Hindus and the Muslims had resulted in civil war in some parts of India. Consequently, in 1947 the newly independent state of India became a predominantly Hindu country, while the Muslims split away from India to form the nation of Pakistan. Shortly after that, in 1948, Mahatma Gandhi was assassinated by a Hindu fanatic who believed that Gandhi was too conciliatory toward the Muslims. The leadership of the new India fell to one of Gandhi's close associates, Jawaharlal Nehru.

Since independence, India has steadily increased agricultural production, thereby forestalling famine, and has also managed to provide health care and educational facilities in many traditionally backward villages. However, the Indians have suffered from several chronic problems. One is periodic political violence. Several national leaders have been assassinated, including Mahatma Gandhi in 1948, Prime Minister Indira Gandhi (unrelated to Mahatma, but the daughter of Nehru) in 1984, and former prime minister Rajiv Gandhi (son of Indira) in 1991. Another problem is the corruption and bribery within the ruling elite. A third is the huge wealth gap between the relatively small urban upper and middle classes and the large numbers of poor people in the villages. A fourth difficulty involves religious hostilities between some Hindus (about 80 percent of the population) and the Muslims in India (about 11 percent). In the 1990s Hindu fundamentalists stirred up religious emotions by claiming that Muslims were getting preferential treatment from the government. Some Hindu-Muslim violence resulted.

Other Asian Nations   A number of other nations also won independence soon after World War II. The United States granted full sovereignty to the Philippines in 1946. In 1948 Burma and Ceylon (later to be named Sri Lanka) became independent, and the British granted independence to the Malaysian Federation in 1957. Later, in 1963, the Malaysian Federation became the state of Malaysia, and in 1965 the city of Singapore withdrew from Malaysia in order to be independent.

Most of the independence struggles mentioned so far were relatively peaceful, but two Asian areas gained independence through prolonged and bloody wars. In Indonesia a nationalist movement led by Achmed Sukarno declared Indonesia's independence from the Netherlands in 1945, but the Dutch sent troops in an effort to restore their control. Only after several years of brutal colonial war did the Dutch finally recognize Indonesian independence in 1949.

An even longer colonial war ensued in the area known as Indochina, which was part of the French Empire. (The major developments in the war over Indochina were recounted in Chapter 1.) Laos, Cambodia, North Vietnam, and South Vietnam became independent in 1954, after local peoples drove the French out of the Indochinese peninsula. At that point began a long struggle between communist North Vietnam and American-supported South Vietnam, a struggle that finally ended in 1975, when the North Vietnamese conquered South Vietnam and forcibly united all of Vietnam into one country. In 1977 Vietnam took control of Laos and late in 1978 conquered Cambodia, replacing the communist tyrant Pol Pot, who had killed over one million Cambodians in the previous three years. In the 1980s the entire area was mired in a poverty that was one result of forty years of warfare and brutality. Political change began to occur in the late 1980s, when Vietnamese troops withdrew from Cambodia. Peace finally came to the area in the 1990s, as the 1993 elections produced a new government in Cambodia. Communist governments continued to dominate Laos and Vietnam.

Political conflict and violence afflicted several other areas in the 1980s. In Sri Lanka (a large island south of India), thousands died as a result of prolonged civil war between the Sinhalese and the Tamils, two peoples who share the island. In the Philippines, the corrupt President Ferdinand Marcos was driven out of the country in 1986. His successor, Corazon Aquino, had to live with major economic problems and a series of attempted military coups against her government, but she remained president until she was succeeded by Fidel Ramos in 1992.

Some Asian nations industrialized and achieved some prosperity in recent decades. In the 1970s the so-called Four Tigers— South Korea, Taiwan, Hong Kong, and Singapore—became "newly industrialized" countries. In the 1980s industrialization spread to parts of Malaysia, Thailand, Indonesia, and the Philippines. This industrialization of smaller nations, combined with the economic strength of Japan and the recent industrial boom in China, turned East Asia into an economic dynamo in the 1990s.

China   The most dramatic story in Asia in the twentieth century is that of an extraordinary revolution in China, home of over one-fifth of the world's population. The story began less than a century ago, at a time when China was weak, poor, and badly governed. China's weakness during the nineteenth century allowed several European nations and the United States to gain important economic concessions, such as control of most Chinese ports and hence of Chinese commerce. Outside influence in China gradually became so great that, in effect, the Chinese government was controlled by foreign powers, even though China was never a part of any one particular empire.

A revolt against foreign control began with the Boxer Rebellion of 1900, in which young Chinese nationalists attempted, unsuccessfully, to drive the foreigners out of China. The Boxer Rebellion was only the beginning. As recounted in Chapter 1, a nationalist movement known as the Guomindong (Kuomintang) overthrew the Manchu rulers in the hope of establishing a more effective, nationalist government in China. Within a few years though, the Guomindong, led by Jiang Jieshi (Chiang Kai-shek), and the Chinese communists were engaged in a fierce civil war for control of China. After decades of civil struggle and after battling the Japanese during World War II, the communists finally gained control of China in 1949.

In recent years the People's Republic of China has developed the Pinyin system for transliteration of Chinese words, and this system is used here. Because most of the works cited in the Suggested Reading use the traditional Wade-Giles system, both forms of the most important names are given below.

Pinyin	Wade-Giles
Beijing	Peking or Peiping
Mao Zedong	Mao Tse-tung
Zhou Enlai	Chou En-lai
Liu Shaoqi	Liu Shao-chi
Deng Xiaoping	Teng Hsiao-p'ing
Lin Biao	Lin Piao
Hua Guofeng	Hua Kuo-feng
Jiang Qing	Chiang Ch'ing
Yanan	Yenan
Jiang Jieshi	Chiang Kai-shek
Guomindong	Kuomintang
Zhao Ziyang	Chao Chi-yang

The new communist government inherited a country that had suffered decades of political and economic turmoil, and by 1949 the economy was near collapse. Furthermore, most Chinese peasants lived in misery and did backbreaking farm work just to survive. The big landowners (less than 10 percent of the population) owned 70 to 80 percent of the land and controlled local governments and financial institutions.

In this situation, the communist regime did what revolutionary governments often do—it sought retribution against its enemies. From 1949 to 1952 between 2 and 5 million people were killed.[4] Some were executed after public trials, but in the countryside many landlords were turned over to irate peasants who either pitchforked them to death or tore them apart. Several million others were imprisoned or sent to forced labor camps. (Death on a large scale was not unusual in China at that time. Untold numbers of Chinese peasants had died of starvation during the first half of the twentieth century, and many others had perished as a result of the civil war and the war with Japan.)

Also in the years after 1949, the Communist party had to consolidate its hold over the political structure. Actually, real power rested in a standing committee of the Party whose five members in 1949 included Mao Zedong (Mao Tse-tung), Zhou Enlai (Chou En-lai), and Liu Shaoqi (Liu Shao-chi). This committee controlled the Party, and since Party members held most key positions in the government, the army, trade unions, the educational system, and all other organizations, the committee controlled the government as well. To give just one example, Mao Zedong was both chairman of the Party and chairman of the government.

The communist leaders quickly set out to transform Chinese society. One of the first measures to be implemented was the marriage law of 1950, which improved the status of women by stipulating that marriage would be based on equality and free mutual consent. Before this, women had been subordinate to men and were often sold into marriage. (Immediately after the marriage law was promulgated, a wave of divorces ensued and in several instances women appeared before a court holding in their arms small children—their future husbands—to whom their families had sold them, well before the boys were of marriageable age.[5]) The marriage law also made it illegal to sell or kill children, previously common with female children. In addition to the marriage law, other reforms were carried out in 1950 and 1951. Opium addiction was forcibly eliminated and organized crime was brought under control, restoring some degree of social order and peace.

Transforming Chinese society was not enough, though. Economic development was essential. In an attempt to improve the lot of the poorest peasants, the new government instituted a wave of agrarian reform which brought peasants into cooperative farms. By 1957 most peasants were members of these cooperatives and slowly started to modernize the agricultural system and increase food production. Industry needed to be modernized as well, and in 1953 the government launched a Five Year Plan designed to develop more heavy industry and increase steel, iron, and coal production.

By the mid-1950s a major policy dispute broke out within the Chinese leadership over the question of the best approach to economic development. Liu Shaoqi, Deng Xiaoping (Teng Hsiaop'ing), and many others emphasized technological development and material progress. They stressed the importance of urban industrialization and centralized economic planning by experts.

Mao Zedong favored what was called the Yanan Way (it was enunciated in the late 1930s when the communist headquarters was in the ancient city of Yanan). This approach emphasized agricultural development and rural industrialization because Mao and his followers believed that the peasants were the natural carriers of revolution. Mao wanted to ensure mass participation by the peasants in order that a social revolution would accompany the economic revolution. (To Mao "mass participation" did not imply political democracy. Rather, it meant that the economic revolution would be carried out by peasants instead of a small number of experts.)[6]

In 1958 the government announced a new drive for industrialization based on Mao's ideas, the "Great Leap Forward." The goal of the Great Leap was simple: the masses of peasants and workers would create an industrial revolution. The Great Leap encouraged peasants and workers to build small "backyard" steel and iron furnaces, but the furnaces were neither efficient nor practical. Other, more effective, measures included small-scale chemical and fertilizer factories and coal mines, most located in rural areas where the products were most needed.

At the same time as the development of this rural industrialization program, another element was introduced: People's Communes. Communes, where peasants or workers would live and work communally, had long been a part of communist ideology. By late 1958 almost all the rural population, plus a very small part of the urban population, was organized into twenty-four thousand People's Communes. The communes averaged about five thousand households and thirty thousand people. Although families did have separate living quarters, work was communal (peasants labored together in production brigades), meals were communal (everyone ate in a common dining hall), and facilities for child care and medical help were operated communally.

The results of the Great Leap Forward and the communal movement were disastrous. In the late 1950s and early 1960s a famine caused largely by the Great Leap killed thirty million to forty million people.

The Great Leap was dismantled by late 1959, and the period from 1960 to 1965 saw a reassertion of the economic approach favored by Liu Shaoqi. Centralized control was reimposed on industrial enterprises. Communes continued to exist, but the peasants were allowed to cultivate private plots of land. Slowly, economic production began to revive, and by the early 1960s production statistics were again increasing.

Mao Zedong refused to give up his vision of peasant socialism (the Yanan Way). He believed that urban industrialization led to inequality, not to egalitarian communism, because it favored experts over the masses, urban workers over peasants, and the cities over the countryside. He and his followers made one more attempt to implement the Yanan Way: the "Great Proletarian Cultural Revolution."

The Cultural Revolution was "cultural" in the sense that Mao Zedong and his followers wanted to transform Chinese civilization and eliminate all capitalist influences from China. They intended to increase the political awareness of the masses through instruction in revolutionary ideals and to purify the Party and the government bureaucracy by sending Party members to the countryside where they would perform manual labor along with the peasants. In short, Mao thought he could remake the Chinese people.

The struggle began in May 1966. The Red Guards, a revolutionary mob composed of high school and college students, held massive rallies in Beijing. Then they began to "investigate" all those suspected of being corrupted by Western, capitalist influences. Some of those being investigated were assaulted and killed; others were sent to labor camps to be "reeducated" or were forced to wear dunce caps in public. Many people were persecuted in one way or another, and millions were killed.[7] The peak of the violence occurred in 1967 and 1968, when different Red Guards factions fought each other over which was displaying the highest degree of revolutionary "ardor." In 1969 Mao Zedong had to call out the army to dismantle the Red Guards and restore public order.

During the upheaval, Mao Zedong achieved much of what he

wanted. Liu Shaoqi (who died in prison in 1969) and other prominent anti-Maoists lost their political positions and disappeared
from the public scene. (Lin Biao, rumored to be the leader of a
potential military coup against Mao, died in a mysterious plane
crash.) Mao completely controlled the Party, and the government
and became almost a minor deity in China. For a time, portraits
and plaster busts were everywhere, and people learned to recite his
sayings. Aside from the virtual deification of Mao, the Cultural
Revolution reinvigorated the rural industrialization program and
produced a major improvement in the health and educational facilities available in rural areas. The price paid for these successes
was that many people were persecuted and/or killed and that the
country was gravely weakened because many educational and scientific institutions were closed or dismantled during the Cultural
Revolution.

By the early 1970s the turmoil of the Cultural Revolution
subsided. At this time Mao Zedong and Zhou Enlai were the dominant political figures. The two leaders began to change Chinese
foreign policy. Since the Sino-Soviet split of the 1960s (discussed in
Chapter 1), the Chinese had come to perceive the Soviet Union as
their major enemy and to think of the United States as a necessary
counterbalance to Soviet power, even though the United States and
China had not maintained diplomatic relations since 1949.

In February 1972 U.S. president Richard Nixon paid a his-
toric visit to China. At the conclusion of his visit, the two nations
announced a desire to normalize their diplomatic relations, and
this was accomplished in 1979. Also in 1972, the Chinese restored
diplomatic relations with Japan, an old enemy from World War II,
and shortly thereafter China gained full membership rights in the
United Nations. (Previously, the UN had recognized the island of
Taiwan, controlled by the old Guomindang forces, as the legitimate
representative of China. The UN position mirrored the position of
the United States and some other major countries, who argued that
the communist government in Beijing was not legitimate. This
argument collapsed in the 1970s.) By the mid-1970s, then, China
had gained new status in the international community as well as
some economic assistance from the outside world.

These foreign policy changes were the last major accomplish-
ments of the generation of leaders who made the Chinese revolution, for in 1976 both Zhou Enlai and Mao Zedong died. They left
behind a fundamental disagreement about how the Chinese revolution should proceed. Almost immediately after Mao Zedong's
death, a power struggle broke out in Beijing. One group, later

branded as the "Gang of Four," wanted to maintain the radical tradition of the Cultural Revolution. Another group, led by Deng Xiaoping and Hua Guofeng (Hua Kuo-feng), favored more stable government and economic policies previously associated with Liu Shaoqi. The Deng-Hua group won the power struggle, and eventually the members of the "Gang of Four" were convicted of various crimes and given long prison sentences. Hua also lost influence after a few years. By the late 1970s the real source of power was Deng.

Since the late 1970s Deng and his followers have encouraged economic modernization while maintaining the Communist party's domination over China. The results of their policies included a major economic boom in the 1980s and 1990s and a significant improvement in the standard of living of some Chinese. They also included a series of major protests against the political tyranny of the Party.

Economic modernization required reducing governmental control over the economy. Agriculture was decollectivized to the extent that peasants could farm their own plots and sell the produce as they saw fit (even though communes still owned the land). The result was improved productivity. Many small shops were allowed to operate free of state control, so small businesses could seek profits in any way they wished. The government encouraged foreign trade and foreign investment for the first time in decades. To stimulate investment, some large industrial enterprises got limited freedom from state control, although many factories remained state-dominated.

During the 1980s and early 1990s the Chinese economy grew by an average of 9 percent a year, and in the mid-1990s it was the fourth-largest economy in the world. Many Chinese who worked in industrial cities (mainly on the South China coast) enjoyed a rising standard of living. In 1990 World Bank figures said that China had a per capita GNP of about $370, but that figure was inaccurate because the statistics did not keep up with China's growth rate. The real GNP per capita was around $1,000 to $1,200, meaning that tens of millions of Chinese were living better than a decade before.[8]

There were problems, however. A growing wealth gap indicated that urban, educated Chinese gained far more from the improving economy than did hundreds of millions of Chinese peasants. Also, rapid industrialization produced severe environmental deterioration, particularly acid rain. Just as China's economic boom is one of the largest in the planet's history (because of the large population involved), so is the environmental problem one of the largest in history.

The economic boom was accompanied by some political and social turmoil. For the common people, a big issue in the 1980s was the government's policy of one child per family. The government, knowing that the country's population was over one billion, tried to curtail population growth by encouraging families to have only one child. Many peasants resisted this policy, the result being that the government forced many pregnant women who already had children to undergo an abortion. Since peasants traditionally prefer having sons, some families responded by killing their female babies so that they would still have the opportunity to have a son. As a result of this peasant resistance, the government relaxed its policy of enforced abortion in the late 1980s.

Opposition to the communist regime also appeared in a series of protests by university students, intellectuals, and other citizens in the major cities. In 1979 a "Democracy Wall" (a wall where posters expressing various opinions were displayed) in Beijing became a center of antigovernment criticism for several months. In 1986 several antigovernment demonstrations occurred in Shanghai. Most serious from the government's perspective was the massive demonstration in Tiananmen Square (near the centers of government in Beijing) in 1989.

In April 1989 university students, later joined by many others, began to protest in Tiananmen Square against corruption within the Communist party (whereby children of Party members often got favored treatment when applying for jobs or admission to universities) and for "democracy." Precisely what the protestors (eventually numbering over a million) meant by democracy was unclear, but a Statue of Democracy was erected in the square and was seen on television throughout the world. For a brief time it appeared that the demonstration might lead to fundamental political change in China. However, in June 1989, Deng Xiaoping, Premier Li Peng, and other hardliners in the Party ordered the army to crush the demonstration. The resulting army attack in Tiananmen Square led to the deaths of hundreds of demonstrators and the wounding of thousands more. In 1990–1991 several captured protestors were executed, and a number of student leaders received long prison sentences. Thus, while communist governments in the Soviet Union and the Eastern European nations were being driven from power, the communist regime in China was forcefully blocking political change so that it could remain in control.

China has endured much revolutionary change and chaos in

the twentieth century, and many millions of Chinese died as a result of that chaos. The Chinese communists brought much suffering and destruction to China, but they also managed to develop an economic system that feeds and clothes nearly a quarter of the world's population. By the mid-1990s a major question was whether the Communist party could maintain its grip on power. The economic boom of the 1980s and 1990s created a lot of social mobility and a rising middle class that, as shown by the Tiananmen Square events, was increasingly unhappy with Party tyranny. The Party and the country could face a crisis when Deng Xiaoping dies (he was ninety in 1994) and new leadership must be selected.

Another issue for the future involves the incorporation of Hong Kong into China. Hong Kong was colonized by Great Britain in the midnineteenth century and since then has developed a thriving capitalist economy, but British treaty rights in the city expire in 1997. At that point, Hong Kong will be rejoined to China, and its capitalist economy will have to be merged somehow with the Chinese communist system.

The Muslim World

Muslims constitute approximately one-fifth of the world's population. The heart of the Muslim world stretches from India westward through Iran to the Mediterranean and then across North Africa. Many of the people who live in this area are Arabs; their religion is Islamic. Some nations, such as Iran, are non-Arabic but adhere to the Islamic faith. There are, in addition, many Muslims in other parts of Africa, parts of Europe and the United States, and in Indonesia.

Several countries in the Muslim world were technically independent before World War II, but in reality most of the area was still controlled by outside powers. France and Great Britain, in particular, dominated the commerce and petroleum resources of the area.

Changes began to occur, however, even before the war was over. In 1944 several Arab states formed the Arab League to encourage Arab unity and to force out foreign powers. Under pressure from the League, Lebanon and Syria became independent in 1944 and British and French forces left the two countries in 1946. Transjordan (later to be named Jordan) also became independent in 1946, and in the same year foreign troops left the nominally independent countries of Iraq and Iran. The story in Egypt was more complex. Technically, Egypt was an independent nation, but

The Middle East

Great Britain controlled the Suez Canal and by that means actually dominated Egyptian commerce and politics. In 1952 a group of nationalistic army officers overthrew Egyptian King Farouk. Eventually Gamal Abdel Nasser became the leader of the new regime, and he ended British domination by establishing Egyptian control over the canal in 1956.

Other Arab states in North Africa also became independent during the 1950s. Freedom came peacefully to Libya in 1951 and to Tunisia and Morocco in 1956. In Algeria, however, the struggle for independence resulted in a brutal war. Algeria, a part of the French Empire, was inhabited predominantly by Arabs, but French settlers controlled the country and were determined to keep Algeria a part of France. Armed struggle became the only way that Algerian Arabs could liberate themselves, and the revolt against French rule began in 1954. The war dragged on until 1962, when Algeria finally received its independence. The price of the war was high for both Algeria and France. Several hundred thousand Algerians died as a result of the war, and in France the war produced so much political turmoil that in 1958 the government collapsed and Charles de Gaulle had to assume power. It was de Gaulle who eventually granted independence to Algeria.

Virtually all Muslim states were independent by the early 1960s. Some of them soon discovered that oil production could make them both wealthy and powerful. The Organization of Petroleum Exporting Countries (OPEC) was formed in 1960 and is dominated by Muslim states, especially Saudi Arabia and some Persian Gulf kingdoms. OPEC raised world oil prices in 1973–1974 and again in 1979–1980, thereby causing a major world recession (see Chapter 2). OPEC's power declined by the 1980s, though, partly because conservation measures reduced world demand for oil and partly because several nations (Great Britain, Norway, India, Brazil) were able to increase their own oil production and reduce dependency on OPEC.

In recent decades, two major wars, both involving Iraq, have erupted in the Muslim world. First was the Iran-Iraq War, which lasted from 1980 to 1989. The two countries came to blows because of border disputes, rivalry for influence in the Persian Gulf, Iraqi fears that Iranian fundamentalists were trying to subvert the Iraqi government, and Iraqi beliefs that Iraq would win easily because Iran was supposedly weakened by its 1979 revolution against the Shah (see below). The war ended indecisively, although more than a million people were killed or wounded. Second was the Persian Gulf War of 1990–1991. In August 1990 Iraqi dictator Saddam Hussein ordered his troops to invade the small nation of Kuwait to gain control of its oil wealth. The United States, fearing that Iraqi domination of Kuwait could produce political and economic instability in an area vital to the world economy, decided to resist Iraq. With limited support from several other nations, the United States sent a large military force to the Persian Gulf, and in January–February 1991 U.S. troops drove the Iraqis out of Kuwait. Few Americans died, but estimates are that over a hundred thousand Iraqi soldiers were killed. Also, the area suffered major environmental damage from air pollution caused by oil wells set ablaze by the Iraqis and by oil spills in the Persian Gulf.

Water may be a source of future conflict in the Muslim world. Several countries in North Africa and the Middle East are already using most of their fresh surface and groundwater, and they cannot accommodate major population growth. Water wars could result, as countries fight over control of underground aquifers or over who is entitled to draw from a river. An obvious possibility would be Israel, Jordan, and the Palestinians fighting for control of the Jordan River; another would be war between Syria and Turkey, which controls the headwaters of rivers that run through Syria.

The Islamic Movement   Since independence, most Arab states have had authoritarian governments in which a secular elite— usually military officers and some civilian politicians—tried to modernize their countries. In the 1970s an Islamic movement, which included some strict Islamic fundamentalists, began to challenge this secular elite.

The Islamic movement originated in opposition to modern secularism (imported from Europe and the United States), which separates religion and politics. The Islamists argue that secularism corrodes moral values and that Islamic law should become the moral and social bases of Islamic societies. The fundamentalists among the Islamists stress strict adherence to a conservative interpretation of the Koran (the Muslim holy book) and want to revive traditional Islamic customs. Some of these customs, such as the subordination of women, raise the question of whether the fundamentalists support religious toleration and human rights for all.

In the 1990s the Islamic movement was often urban-based, with strong appeal to the middle and lower-middle classes. Many university graduates and young professionals were Islamists, indicating that many of those with modern educations were disenchanted with secularism. Most of the Islamists were moderate-minded people who wanted to Islamize their societies through religious education and elections. These moderates were often physicians, lawyers, and teachers who worked in Islamic hospitals, legal aid offices, and educational institutions and believed that their societies could be modernized without sacrificing traditional Islamic values. Some of the Islamists were more radical and often used violent methods against their enemies.[9]

The first political breakthrough for the Islamic movement was the Libyan revolution of 1969, which brought Mu'ammar Gaddafi to power. Since 1969 Gaddafi has supported various revolutionary and terrorist groups in an attempt to export Islamic revolution. A second breakthrough occurred in Iran. In the decades after World War II, the Shah of Iran (who was not a devout Muslim) sought to carry out a massive economic development program, but the development occurred too rapidly and produced too many economic and social disruptions. The resulting discontent led to the Shah's overthrow in 1979. He eventually took refuge in the United States and his government was replaced by an Islamic republic, in which fundamentalists led by the Ayatollah Ruhollah Khomeini were the controlling element. The new government saw the United States, the Shah's old ally, as the great enemy. Iranian students held the staff of the American embassy in Iran hostage from November 1979 until January 1981, largely because the United States refused to return the Shah, whom many Iranians regarded as a criminal, to Iran to stand trial for his alleged crimes.

The Islamic movement continued to dominate Libya and Iran in the mid-1990s, although in Iran high inflation and unemployment produced growing popular resentment against the fundamentalist rulers. Fundamentalism also prevailed in Saudi Arabia. In several other countries, Islamists were the strongest opposition to the ruling elite. The Islamic Salvation Front won the December 1991 parliamentary elections in Algeria, but the military government annulled the elections. Neither the Algerian military nor the fundamentalists were committed to democratic principles, so in the mid-1990s Algeria remained divided between two authoritarian political forces. In Egypt, President Husni Mubarek's regime faced a growing Islamist opposition that sometimes resorted to terrorism. (Mubarek's predecessor, President Anwar Sadat, was assassinated by Muslim extremists in 1981.) The wide income gap between the rich and the poor in Egypt was one element that increased the popularity of the Islamic opposition.

The Arab-Israeli Conflict   The most enduring conflict in the Muslim world is the prolonged struggle between the Arabs and the Israelis for control of the area traditionally known as Palestine. For centuries Palestine was inhabited primarily by Arabs who naturally regarded the area as theirs. Yet in biblical days, Palestine had been the homeland of the Jewish people. In the nineteenth century, growing numbers of Jews from around the world embraced Zionism, a nationalist movement which sought to establish a national Jewish state in Palestine. The Zionist movement grew rapidly in the twentieth century, when Nazi Germany launched what Jews came to call the "Holocaust," meaning, literally, sacrificed or destroyed by fire. Between 1941 and 1945, the Nazis murdered at least six million Jews, whom they branded as racial enemies. (The Nazis also murdered several million other people, including gypsies, invalids, Poles, Russians, homosexuals, and political opponents.) To escape from this nightmare, more and more Jews immigrated to Palestine in hopes of building a state that would become a haven for all Jews. This emigration was resisted by the British, who, under a mandate from the League of Nations, controlled Palestine between the two world wars. It was also resisted by the Arabs, who considered Palestine to be their homeland and, in addition, felt entitled to control many of the religious shrines in the area. All three groups—the British, Jews, Arabs—often resorted to violence to gain their ends.

After World War II, the British turned the Palestinian controversy over to the United Nations. The UN voted to partition Palestine into Arab and Jewish states of roughly equal size. Both Jews and Arabs rejected the UN plan, and in 1948 the Jewish population unilaterally proclaimed the new state of Israel. Immediately, the surrounding Arab nations invaded Israel in what became know as the War of the Arab League, but a ragtag Israeli army defeated the Arabs, who were disunited and poorly prepared.

During the war the Israelis conquered more land than the UN had allotted to them, and ever since the Arabs have demanded the return of this land. Many of the Arabs in Palestine (Palestinians) were driven out or fled their homes in panic during the war, and after the Arab defeat many of them were forced to settle in squalid refugee camps near Israel. The Palestinians wanted to return to their homes, but the Israelis refused, because some Palestinians demanded the destruction of the new Israeli state and also because many Israelis did not want a large Arab population in Israel.

Since 1948 the Palestinians, many still living in refugee camps in countries near Israel, have become violent opponents of Israel. In 1964 the *Palestine Liberation Organization* (PLO) was formed as a resistance movement among the refugees, and the PLO (headed by Yasir Arafat) led the struggle to restore Palestine to Arab control. With the support of several Arab states, the Palestinians continually launched guerrilla attacks against Israel. Full-scale wars erupted four times. In 1956 Israel invaded Egypt in conjunction with Great Britain and France, who wanted to regain control of the Suez Canal, but the invaders withdrew under pressure from the United Nations and the United States. In the Six Day War of 1967, Israel invaded and conquered more Arab territory, including the West Bank and East Jerusalem, taken from Jordan, the Golan Heights, taken from Syria, and the Gaza Strip and the Sinai Peninsula, taken from Egypt. In 1973, during the Yom Kippur War, the Muslim states used oil price increases and an oil embargo to force the United States and the Western European states to pressure Israel into being more accommodating toward the Arabs.

In 1977 President Anwar Sadat of Egypt visited Israel in an effort to hasten a Middle East settlement. With the strong support of President Jimmy Carter of the United States, Egypt and Israel concluded a peace agreement in 1978, and the Sinai Peninsula was returned to Egypt. Most Muslims, however, continued to oppose Israel, and war broke out again in 1982 when Israel invaded Lebanon in a successful attempt to drive the PLO out of the country and far away from Israeli borders. Lebanon was already suffering from a civil war between Muslim and Christian groups. The civil war and the Israeli invasion combined to destroy the effectiveness of the Lebanese government, so Lebanon became a chaotic place where bloodshed and terror reigned. Eventually, the Syrian army intervened, becoming de facto occupiers of Lebanon.

In 1987 began the *intifada*, an uprising by Palestinians living in the Israeli-controlled West Bank and Gaza area. The Palestinians precipitated small-scale riots and much passive resistance in a prolonged campaign to disrupt Israeli domination of Palestinians.

A major breakthrough occurred in September 1993, when after two years of negotiations the PLO and Israel signed a mutual recognition agreement. The underlying principle of the agreement was that the PLO recognized the right to existence of the Jewish state of Israel in exchange for an Israeli acceptance of the right of Palestinians to some form of self-rule. In practice, the agreement granted the PLO limited autonomy in governing two small areas populated by Palestinians, the Gaza Strip (a small strip of land along the southeastern coast of the Mediterranean) and the town of Jericho in the West Bank. Early in 1994 the PLO assumed authority in the two areas. It confronted major problems, one being the desperate poverty of the two areas and another being the fact that the PLO (hitherto a resistance organization) had no experience at governing. Nevertheless, future negotiations to expand Palestinian self-rule were planned.

Some extremists on boths sides opposed the 1993 agreement. Jewish extremists opposed it because they want to keep all of Israel under Jewish control and refuse to accept any Palestinian rights to self-government within the existing borders of Israel. Arab extremists continue to want to destroy Israel and return the entire area to Arab control. However, two basic facts, one on each side, impelled the PLO and the Israelis to make peace. One was that the PLO and Palestinians lacked the power to destroy Israel, so they had to compromise to gain anything. The other was that Israel felt it had to end a situation in which its Jewish population (three to four million in the early 1990s) tried to control almost two million increasingly hostile Palestinians.

The Israeli-PLO agreement was followed by other peace negotiations in the area. In July 1994 Israel and Jordan agreed to end formally the state of war that had existed between the two since 1948, and a few months later they announced plans to restore diplomatic relations. A further development at the end of 1994 was the possibility of peace talks between Israel and Syria.

Sub-Saharan Africa

The decolonization process in sub-Saharan Africa began in the mid-1950s. In 1957 Ghana, led by Kwame Nkrumah, attained independence. In 1960 Nigeria achieved statehood, but it experienced political turmoil and civil war during the 1960s. Also in 1960, the Belgian Congo (later named Zaire) became independent, but quickly collapsed into a civil war that lasted until 1965. The new state of Tanganyika, led by Julius Nyerere, was born in 1961; in 1964 Tanganyika united with Zanzibar to become the state of Tanzania. Many other states gained independence in the 1960s. By the end of the decade the British, French, Belgian, and Spanish empires had virtually disappeared from the African continent.

Several of the nations mentioned above attained independence relatively easily, but other areas had to endure long struggles to become independent. Parts of southern and eastern Africa contained substantial populations of white settlers who resisted any independence movement that might lead to black majority rule. In Kenya the struggle for independence from white domination lasted throughout most of the 1950s. Not until 1963 was a black-ruled Kenya established, under the leadership of Jomo Kenyatta.

In Southern Rhodesia, a white-dominated minority government declared independence from Great Britain in 1965. The Rhodesian whites resisted black guerrilla forces for over a decade, but in 1980 Southern Rhodesia became the black-controlled state of Zimbabwe, led by Robert Mugabe. Long colonial wars also occurred in Angola and Mozambique, until, in 1975, these two countries won their independence from Portugal.

Since achieving independence, most of the new states in sub-Saharan Africa have faced many problems. One is a chronic political instability that often leads to establishment of despotic governments. When the colonial powers left Africa, they usually made little effort to prepare the Africans for independence or for democratic government. Furthermore, most of the African nations are nations in name only. The boundaries of the new states were drawn in the nineteenth century to suit the convenience of the colonial powers, the result being that these states contain many diverse ethnic groups who may or may not be accustomed to cooperating with each other. Hence, it is almost inevitable for these new nations to experience civil wars and social disorder, as the various groups fight among themselves for political power and economic wealth. Often the only source of national unity is the army, so in many instances the military has seized political power in an attempt to maintain some semblance of social order.[10] A few military governments have ruled effectively, but most have not. One of the worst military regimes appeared in Uganda in the 1970s, when the dictator Idi Amin and his forces murdered two or three hundred thousand people before Tanzania invaded and overthrew him in 1979.

In the 1980s and 1990s more than a dozen states in sub-Saharan Africa endured long civil wars. In Angola, war between two groups fighting for control of the country lasted from 1975 into the 1990s and resulted in the deaths of several hundred thousand people. In Sudan, a war between Muslims in the north and non-Muslims in the south began in 1983, continued through the 1980s, and eventually produced a famine in which nearly half a million died. Mozambique had a civil war from 1976 to 1992 that killed almost a million people. Most recently, civil war erupted in Rwanda in 1994, with hundreds of thousands being murdered in cold blood. These and many other examples that could be given illustrate the brutality that results when basic social order collapses.

A second problem is the desperate poverty that afflicts sub-Saharan Africa. At the time of independence in the 1950s and 1960s, Africa was the poorest region on earth, and average per capita income in the new states was usually less than $100 a year.[11] However, some progress occurred after independence. Between 1960 and 1980 school enrollments in Africa grew dramatically, life expectancy rose from thirty-nine to forty-seven years, and many construction projects, such as roads and ports, were completed.[12] Despite these accomplishments, sub-Saharan Africa was the poorest region on earth in the 1980s, as population grew faster than food production. By 1990 thirty-two of the world's forty poorest countries were African. Among several basic reasons for the failure of the African economy are the following: (1) The colonial legacy undermined Africa from the beginning, as many African states (formed by the colonial powers) are so small that they are unlikely

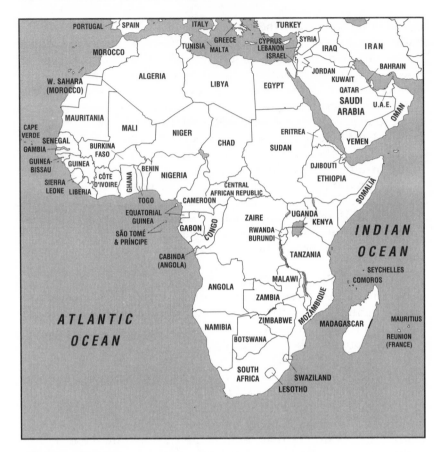

Africa in the 1990s

to ever be economically viable. Six African nations have populations of less than a million, and the populations of nineteen nations
are less than five million. (2) African governments did not perform
well after independence. Civil wars often destroyed economies and
sometimes induced famines. Even when governments were stable,
they often undermined food production by enforcing low agricultural prices in order to guarantee cheap food for urban populations. (3) The African climate produces poor soil in many areas,
and tropical conditions encourage the spread of diseases. (4) Refugees from wars and economic disasters overwhelm economic structures and social order in many parts of Africa.[13]

A good example of economic failure is the nation of Zaire,
which has enough valuable raw materials (rubber, cobalt, indus-

trial diamonds) to be very prosperous. In 1960 Zaire (then known as the Belgian Congo) won its independence from Belgium, but the Belgians deliberately left no indigenous political or economic leadership in Zaire. The result was civil war from 1960 to 1965, at which point the army, led by General Joseph Mobutu, seized control of the government. Since then, the Mobutu regime has siphoned off much of the country's wealth for the benefit of a small elite and left most of the population living in desperate poverty. By the mid-1990s the Zairean government (still nominally headed by Mobutu) and economy were collapsing into chaos.

In addition to political and economic problems, other factors exacerbate Africa's plight. Most African women are poorly educated, subservient to men, and therefore unable to function as full participants in their societies. An AIDS (Acquired Immune Deficiency Syndrome) epidemic infected an estimated ten million people in sub-Saharan Africa by the early 1990s and overwhelmed medical facilities in many areas. The natural environment is deteriorating as overuse of land intensifies the desertification problem, particularly along the southern edge of the Sahara Desert, and contributes to deforestation in several areas. Much African wildlife is being decimated; for example, large numbers of elephants are killed by hunters who can make huge profits selling elephant tusks to ivory merchants. Many nations, including the United States, have banned ivory imports in an attempt to stop the slaughtering of elephants, but an illegal ivory trade continues.

All these problems led to incredible hardship for many Africans in the 1970s, 1980s, and 1990s. A story told by a Red Cross food-relief worker about a young boy and his mother illustrated the nightmare of extreme poverty: "This is Kiros. When he came in here two months ago he was so starved that he was like a skeleton. His mother kept hitting him [out of frustration] and he kept asking her why."[14]

Despite all the terrible problems, there are some positive developments in sub-Saharan Africa. Many peasants and small businessmen are resourceful enough to survive and even prosper. Some entire countries are thriving. Botswana, for example, has had a healthy economy and a democratic government for nearly thirty years. A few nations—Nigeria, Zambia, Zimbabwe—were able to increase food production in the 1980s and thus avert the worst effects of the food crisis.

In the late 1980s and early 1990s some political change began to occur. Several dictators were overthrown—for example, Samuel Doe in Liberia in 1990 and Mengistu Haile Mariam in

Ethiopia in 1991. In several other countries, large popular demonstrations for more democratic government led to multiparty elections. A sixteen-year-long civil war in Angola began to subside, as the combatants agreed to a truce in 1991. Another long civil war ended in Mozambique in 1992. (One cause of these political changes was the end of the Cold War between the superpowers. By the late 1980s, both superpowers were withdrawing support from some African despots they had been aiding.)

An important sign of strength in Africa is the fact that African artists and social theorists continue to criticize the failures of the present and to remind their fellow Africans of valuable African traditions. For example, Nigerian Chinua Achebe has written a series of five novels, in which he examines with humor and insight the story of Nigeria in the twentieth century. The first in the series, *Things Fall Apart* (1958), explores the disintegration of traditional Nigerian society after the British colonialists took control of the country. The last, *Anthills of the Savannah* (1987), criticizes the corrupt military governments that dominated Nigeria for most of the years after independence.

South Africa Particularly dramatic changes occurred in South Africa, the last white-dominated state on the African continent. White people—some of English descent and others known as Afrikaners of Dutch descent—have controlled the country throughout the twentieth century even though they comprise less than 20 percent of the population.

The Afrikaners dominated the government after 1948 and imposed a policy of "apartheid" (racial separation) on South Africa. Apartheid forbade interracial marriage, prevented blacks from participating in national political life, forced each race to live in separate well-defined areas, and limited employment and educational opportunities for blacks. The blacks opposed apartheid, and the African National Congress (ANC) became the organization of black opposition. By the 1980s a simmering race war developed. Blacks protested and rioted against the white government and the government responded by imprisoning and killing some blacks. The South African problem became an international political issue, since many African nations supported the protests of South African blacks and some of the Western, industrialized nations established economic sanctions against South Africa in an attempt to force political change. By the late 1980s, the South African economy was suffering.

These pressure tactics plus the collapse of communism in

Nelson Mandela casting his vote at Ohlange High School in Inanda, near Durban, April 27, 1994, in South Africa's first all-race elections. Mandela became president of South Africa as a result of the election.

SOURCE: Peter Dejong/ AP/Wide World Photos.

Europe, which seemed to show how quickly a governmental system could crumble, encouraged the South African government to begin dismantling the apartheid system. In 1990 President Frederik W. de Klerk released ANC leader Nelson Mandela from prison and legalized the previously outlawed ANC and other antiapartheid organizations. In 1991 de Klerk, pressured by Mandela and many others, announced that the government intended to repeal all apartheid laws. For example, new legislation allowed black and white children to attend school together.

Through the early 1990s de Klerk and Mandela led talks among all the major political factions; the talks gradually resulted in a negotiated agreement to end white domination of South Africa. In April 1994 the first universal suffrage election in South African history was held. The election produced a government that for the first time included both blacks and whites, and Nelson Mandela became the first black president of South Africa.

The new government faced many problems. Extremists among both blacks and whites threatened violence. Furthermore, the residue of apartheid had to be overcome, as blacks had far less access than whites to good jobs, educational opportunity, housing, and medical care. Still, a remarkable breakthrough had occurred.

After centuries of racial separation and fear, most South African whites, led by de Klerk, agreed relatively peacefully to relinquish white domination and accept a government largely controlled by the majority blacks. The blacks were led by people, most notably Mandela, who wanted to build a democratic South Africa and apparently bore relatively little animosity against the whites.

Latin America

Because most Latin American countries attained their political independence in the nineteenth century, decolonization has not been a significant issue in recent decades. The major issues in this part of the world are economic and social. The population of Latin America has greatly increased in the twentieth century, and by the mid-1990s at least two-thirds of the population lived in urban areas. Economic production has not kept up with the population increase. Consequently, most Latin Americans are poor, while an elite few are wealthy. Many of the poor are peasants, who have little or no land to farm. Others live in urban shantytowns, large areas of tents and shacks that can contain hundreds of thousands of people who lack such basics as clean water. Shantytowns surround many of the largest cities, such as Mexico City and Rio de Janeiro in Brazil. Adults in the towns may spend hours each day commuting to and from low-paying jobs. Children often live in the streets, surviving as best they can while their parents are gone.[15]

By contrast, a small wealthy class usually dominates government and society in Latin American nations. Hence, a major issue throughout Latin America is what can and should be done about the immense gap between the minority rich and the majority poor.

Economic Development   During the 1970s, 1980s, and early 1990s a variety of economic problems dominated most Latin American societies. Inflation plagued many countries, particularly Argentina, Brazil, and Peru. Foreign debt was a major issue for some, as Mexico and Brazil, for example, found it increasingly difficult to make debt payments. Civil wars undermined the economies of Nicaragua and El Salvador. In Peru, Bolivia, and Colombia, impoverished peasants tried to survive by cultivating coca, which was then processed into cocaine for sale in the United States and Western Europe.

The need for economic development has encouraged a few nations—Brazil, Mexico, Chile—to greatly increase industrial production. Brazil exports large amounts of steel, chemicals, and machinery, while Mexico sells many automobiles and textiles. But even these relatively well-off nations contain large numbers of impoverished people, and most other countries are even poorer.

One approach to encouraging economic growth is the formation of free-trade areas to stimulate commerce among nations. In 1991 the members of the Andean Pact—Venezuela, Bolivia, Chile, Colombia, Ecuador, and Peru—agreed to remove all tariffs among them and to form an Andean Common Market by 1995. Also in 1991, the Central American trade group agreed to gradually integrate the economies of the members—Mexico, Guatemala, El Salvador, Honduras, Nicaragua, and Costa Rica. In addition, the United States, Canada, and Mexico created NAFTA, the North American Free Trade Agreement, in 1994.

However, the socioeconomic problem got worse in the 1980s and early 1990s. According to UN statistics, 44 percent of Latin Americans lived at poverty levels in the early 1990s, an increase of 3 percent compared with the 1970s. The free-trade and industrialization programs benefited primarily the upper and middle classes, not the lower classes. For example, in Brazil, Peru, and Ecuador in the early 1990s, the wealthiest 20 percent of families earned thirty times more per year than did the poorest 20 percent of families.[16] Another example was the "street children"—at least two million children who wandered the streets of various Latin American cities and tried to survive through petty crime, prostitution, and the drug trade.

The case of Haiti illustrates the plight of the Latin American poor. From 1957 to 1986 Haiti was controlled by the Duvalier family, who used private armies to brutally enforce their authority. Most Haitians were impoverished. In 1986 violent riots drove out the last Duvalier, and in 1990 the first free elections in decades sent to the presidency Jean-Bertrand Aristide, a charismatic slum priest who promised to improve the lot of the poor. He was overthrown in 1991 by an army coup, supported by the conservative business classes and criminal gangs. The UN, pressured by the United States and others, applied economic sanctions against the antidemocratic military government; at the same time, tens of thousands of Haitian refugees sought to escape to the United States by sailing across the Caribbean in dilapidated vessels. In September 1994 U.S. troops occupied Haiti, forced the military leaders to relinquish power, and then reinstalled Aristide as president. He faced major problems of poverty, environmental decline, and deep social divisions between the small but wealthy elite and the impoverished majority of the population. U.N. forces replaced U.S. occupation troops in the spring of 1995.

The struggle for economic development has led to severe environmental degradation in some places. In El Salvador, for example, thousands of acres of land have been deforested and eroded by peasants trying to cultivate marginal farmland. Particularly significant is the Brazilian attempt to develop the Amazon Basin, which is a treasure house of natural resources. The basin covers 2 million square miles and contains vast quantities of iron ore, bauxite, gold, nickel, copper, and timber. But the Amazon is a tropical rain forest, and its ecosystem is very fragile. In tropical rain forests, the soil is thin because the trees, with their massive root structures, soak up most of the nutrients. A growing number of the Amazon's trees have been removed to make room for cattle ranches or mining activities or to supply logging operations. As this happens, many of the nutrients in the forest are lost, and what soil is left can easily disappear through erosion or be baked into desert by high tropical temperatures.[17] If the Amazon is exploited unmercifully, there could potentially be a major ecological disaster. If Brazil manages the economic development of the Amazon carefully, then the Amazon could play a significant role in helping the country overcome its economic difficulties.

Political Developments   Political reactions to the gap between the rich and the poor have usually taken three forms: (1) conservative, authoritarian governments dominated by the military and the wealthy upper classes; (2) civilian, semidemocratic governments; and (3) Marxist revolutionary regimes.

Military forces have often seized control of Latin American nations in order to sustain the power of the upper classes and to repress social unrest in the lower classes. For example, General Augusto Pinochet and the Chilean military controlled Chile from 1973 to 1990. In Brazil, a succession of generals representing the army governed from 1964 to 1985. These and other military governments often used torture and violence against those who opposed them. The Brazilian military tortured to death at least several hundred people, sometimes using a device known as the "dragon chair" in which a prisoner received electric shocks while a dentist's drill shattered his or her teeth.[18]

Civilian rule is usually somewhat more democratic than military government, although rarely representative of the poor classes. Civilian governments replaced military regimes in Argentina in 1983, Brazil in 1985, Chile in 1990, and other nations such as Mexico, Colombia, and Venezuela have a relatively long tradition of civilian control. By the early 1990s, most Latin American nations were free of military dictators, although in 1992 Peruvian president Alberto Fujimori suspended Peru's democratic constitution and began to rule by decree.

In a few places, Marxist groups claiming to represent the poor attained power. In 1959 Fidel Castro came to power in Cuba and installed a Marxist regime that was dictatorial but that provided better health care and working conditions for most of the Cuban people. The Marxist Salvador Allende tried to install a socialist society in Chile after he was elected president in 1970, but he was killed in the 1973 coup that led to the Pinochet military government. A Marxist group known as the Sandinistas led a revolution against the corrupt Somoza government in Nicaragua and achieved power in 1979. However, the Sandinistas were voted out of office in 1990. Also, in the 1980s, Marxist groups tried unsuccessfully to overthrow the government in El Salvador, but the Salvadorean civil war ended in 1992. In all four of these cases, Marxist revolution seemed to many to be the best hope for improving the lives of the common people. Yet, the appeal of Marxism declined in the late 1980s partly because of the collapse of Soviet communism, and in the early 1990s the Castro regime in Cuba was the only Marxist government left in Latin America. Cuba was close to economic breakdown in the mid-1990s.

Religion   Historically, Latin America has been a "Catholic continent," with the church's hierarchy being conservative and supportive of the established social order. In the 1960s, however, a few Catholic intellectuals began to argue that the church should speak out in behalf of the poor and oppressed. The result was "liberation theology," a teaching that Christianity should liberate people from economic poverty as well as from spiritual sin. In some countries—for example, Brazil, Nicaragua, and El Salvador—many parish priests worked in small communities to help the poor achieve both spiritual peace and economic betterment. In the 1980s Pope John Paul II began to restrict the influence of liberation theology because he believed it encouraged Marxist social and economic policies. Yet, liberation theology remained vibrant in the 1990s; for example, Catholic organizations in Bolivia, Venezuela, and Guatemala took strong stands on behalf of the poor.

In the 1980s and 1990s, Catholicism was challenged by the spread of evangelical Protestantism, which often appealed to those moving from country to city in search of work and thereby breaking loose from traditional family and religious ties. Particularly popular in Brazil and Guatemala were Pentecostal churches that practiced faith healing and speaking in tongues; Mormons and Jehovah's Witnesses expanded in other areas. Some of the new Protestant churches were small, urban, store-front groups, while others were large and wealthy, an example being Brazil's Universal Church of the Kingdom of God, which had a $45-million television studio and a radio network.

In the mid-1990s most Latin Americans remained Catholic, but in some areas the appeal of evangelical Protestantism was growing.

Mexico   The recent history of Mexico reveals some of the problems and possibilities in Latin American nations. Mexico is similar to most other Latin American nations in that it suffers from a sharp division between the minority rich and the majority poor. It is different in that Mexico shares a common border with the United States, a fact that continues to shape the history of both countries.

A great event in twentieth-century Mexican history was the revolution of 1910–1920. Before 1910 Mexico was dominated by the dictator Porfirio Díaz, who was supported by the traditional elite—the army, large landowners, the Catholic hierarchy—and by foreign investors, primarily from the United States. The lower classes were impoverished and oppressed, with 95 percent of the rural population owning little or no land. (Fewer than two hundred wealthy families owned a quarter of the farmland, and foreign investors controlled another quarter.)[19] The revolution began with middle-class opposition to the Díaz dictatorship, but workers and peasants soon rebelled as well, and Díaz was forced into exile in 1911. For the next few years, Mexico was in turmoil. In the south, Emiliano Zapata led a peasant rebellion demanding land reform, and he became a popular hero. Pancho Villa led lower-class armies in the north and launched a number of raids into Texas and New Mexico (which some Mexicans believed rightfully belonged to Mexico). Neither could establish an effective national government, however, and in 1920 a new elite (more liberal than the old elite that had supported Díaz) formed a new government and ended the revolution in which over one million Mexicans had been killed. This new elite, composed of middle-class businesspeople and moderately conservative landowners, claimed to support the revolutionary goals of socioeconomic development for the lower classes and national freedom from foreign interference, particularly from the United States.

Since 1920 one political party, led by the new elite and known after 1946 as the Institutional Revolutionary Party has dominated Mexico's government. The party carried out some reforms. In the 1920s a major educational program made some progress in combating illiteracy among the lower classes. In the 1930s Lazaro Cardenas, who was president from 1934 to 1940, became immensely popular as he accelerated the redistribution of land to poor peasants and nationalized the oil companies owned primarily by foreigners. The artist Diego Rivera (1886–1957) expressed the growing pride of Mexicans when, in the 1920s, he painted grand wall murals celebrating Mexican history at the National Palace and the National University, both in Mexico City.

After 1940 the governing elite became more conservative, and the Institutional Revolutionary Party became an instrument whereby wealthy businesspeople and landowners controlled unions and the peasantry. Elections were managed so that only candidates from the dominant party had a real chance of winning. (For example, the government controlled the major television facilities and thus could determine which candidates got television exposure.) A result of the one-party system was that corruption and favoritism came to prevail at all levels of Mexican government.

Those who are politically powerful are also economically powerful. Mexico experienced some economic growth in recent decades and in the 1990s was considered a "middle-income" country rather than one of the desperately poor nations. But the wealth, much of it generated by the sale of oil in the 1970s and early 1980s, was in the hands of a small group of investors and businesspeople. In the countryside, a relatively few large landowners controlled large agricultural enterprises that produced crops for export, particularly to the United States. Millions of peasants had little or no land, and urban unemployment was high. Mexico in the 1980s and 1990s was a country where one-fifth of the population lived well, and four-fifths lived in poverty.

Unemployed workers and landless peasants migrate in search of work. Sometimes they migrate to Mexico City, the capital, where they live in shantytowns and usually remain unemployed or underemployed. Mexico City had a population of 345,000 in 1900, but by 1990 the figure was 15 million. If growth continues as expected, Mexico City may be one of the largest cities in the world by the year 2000, with a population of nearly 20 million and one of the world's worst smog problems.

The other destination for Mexican migrants is the southwestern United States. Both legal and illegal migrants cross the border to take jobs that most Americans regard as low-paying but that many Mexicans see as a step toward a better future. (An anti-immigrant backlash erupted in the November 1994 elections in California, as voters approved a referendum that would prevent illegal immigrants from gaining access to most state services, including education.) The Mexican-U.S. border is one of the few places in the world where a rich nation is directly contiguous with a relatively poor nation, and one result is continuous migration. Another is a large drug trade, in which Mexicans smuggle drugs for sale to affluent Americans.

In recent years, Mexican leaders have encountered growing opposition from the middle and lower classes and so have tried to develop some reforms to address Mexico's social and economic problems. Usually, the reforms were designed to increase manufacturing production and commerce rather than to address directly the inequities in Mexican society. Carlos Salinas de Gortari became president of Mexico in 1988. He directed a large-scale privatization program whereby most of Mexico's state-owned industries were sold to private investors or were merged with private companies. The goal was to make Mexican businesses more efficient and productive. He also led Mexico into NAFTA, the North American Free Trade Agreement with the United States and Canada, which went into effect in 1994. NAFTA is designed to phase out 99 percent of all tariffs over ten years, the hope being that increased trade will benefit all three countries. A continuing problem is likely to be environmental degradation along the U.S.-Mexico border, since water resources are not adequate for the growing population and for agriculture in the area and since expanding industrialization stimulated by NAFTA may well increase air pollution. Another is that lower wage scales in Mexico may tempt U.S. firms to relocate there and thus eliminate jobs held by U.S. workers.

Some in the Mexican lower classes fear that NAFTA and the privatization program will benefit primarily the upper and middle classes. On January 1, 1994, the Zapatista National Liberation Army (a lower-class guerrilla army named for Emiliano Zapata, a leader of the 1910–1920 revolution) attacked several towns and army barracks in the southern state of Chiapas. The Zapatistas demanded more democratic elections and social reforms to provide more jobs, housing, and education for the poor. Their rebellion ended quickly after peace talks with the government, but this outbreak of popular discontent showed that the governing elite continued to lose support among the lower classes.

In the elections of August 1994 Ernesto Zedillo Ponce de León,

Some 1,000 Members of the opposition Revolutionary Democratic Party (a part of the Zapatista movement) from Chiapas camp out in the main plaza of the state capital of Tuxtla Gutierrez, December 7, 1994. The demonstrators were there to protest the swearing in of the ruling PRI governor-elect Eduardo Robledo. "Death to Robledo" graffiti can be seen scrawled on the base of a statue in the plaza.

SOURCE: Joe Cavaretta/AP/Wide World Photos.

the candidate of the Institutional Revolutionary Party, was chosen to succeed Salinas as president, but he won only 50 percent of the vote and thus had the lowest level of electoral support of any ruling party candidate since 1929. In late 1994 and early 1995, Zedillo faced a major financial crisis, in which a precipitous decline in the value of the Mexican currency helped produce economic depression.

THE QUEST FOR ECONOMIC DEVELOPMENT

Most people who have lived on this planet have been poor, and that remains true today. In the twentieth century, poverty still afflicts large numbers of people, particularly in Asia, Africa, and Latin America. However, industrialization has gradually produced the hope that for the first time in history the majority of people on earth could enjoy a decent material standard of living. As Arnold Toynbee, the noted historian, once observed:

> For the first time since the dawn of civilization about 5000 years ago, the masses have now become alive to the possibility that their traditional way of life might be changed for the better. . . . This awakening of hope and purpose in the hearts and minds of the hitherto depressed three-fourths of the world's population will, I feel, stand out in retrospect as the epoch-making event of our age.[20]

There are many criteria for measuring economic development, such as equity in income distribution or infant mortality and life expectancy rates. A standard criterion is GNP per capita, a statistic that shows roughly the average amount of wealth per person in a given country. (The statistics take two or three years to compile and so are always out of date.) According to 1991 World Bank figures, several of the wealthy industrialized nations had a GNP per capita over $20,000, examples being the United States ($22,240) and Germany ($23,650). The newly industrialized countries (NICs)—Singapore, Hong Kong, South Korea, Indonesia, Taiwan, and a few others—have greatly improved their GNP per capita in recent decades, so that, for example, Singapore was at $14,210 and Hong Kong at $13,430 in 1991. Most of the NICs are relatively small Asian states, which concentrate on producing consumer goods or components for high-technology instruments. The developing, or middle-income, countries include nations like Bra-

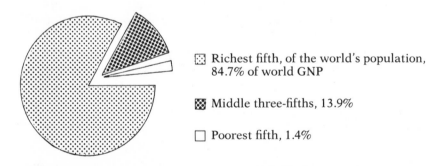

Richest fifth, of the world's population, 84.7% of world GNP

Middle three-fifths, 13.9%

Poorest fifth, 1.4%

Distribution of Global Income, 1991   Wide disparities in income exist both between and within nations.

SOURCE: United Nations Development Program, *Human Development Report, 1993.*

zil ($2,940), Mexico ($3,030), and South Africa ($2,560). These nations usually have an industrial or commercial sector that enables some of the population to live well, but they also have large numbers of poor people, and so the average GNP is relatively low. The least-developed, or poor, countries are those in which all but a tiny elite live in debilitating poverty. Examples include Haiti ($370), Bangladesh ($220), and Ethiopia ($120). Obviously, the gap between the poor nations and the wealthy nations is enormous.[21]

The Problems of Poverty

Even in the poorest countries, some people in the upper classes are relatively well off. Furthermore, the poor nations as a whole have made significant economic progress in recent decades. Since 1950 educational facilities in the poor nations have expanded greatly, health care programs have controlled many diseases and alleviated much suffering, and economic output has increased significantly. Yet, hundreds of millions of people in Asia, Africa, and Latin America still live in poverty, daily confronting the following (and many other) problems.

Population Growth   Just after World War II, world population was over 2 billion. In 1994 the estimated world population was 5.6 billion, with a quarter of a million people being added every day. World Bank estimates are that world population will exceed 6 billion by the year 2000 and 8 billion by 2025.[22] These growing numbers of people are overwhelming and will continue to overwhelm available living resources in many parts of the world.

Most of the population growth is occurring and will occur in Third World nations, because improved medical care and disease prevention techniques lower the death rate in those countries. Asia is the most populous region, with China and India containing about 40 percent of the world's population in the mid-1990s. Sub-Saharan Africa is having the greatest difficulty feeding an expanding population.

If the past is a reliable guide, population pressure could result in a continued exodus from the country to towns and cities. Since most rural villages cannot employ an increasing number of peasants, people seek work in the urban areas. Third World cities may continue to absorb huge numbers of rural migrants, most of whom live in shantytowns and cannot find steady employment.

Some hope exists that population expansion will taper off in the twenty-first century. In recent decades, the rate of world population increase has begun to decline, primarily for two reasons. First, better education and contraceptive techniques allow parents, particularly women, to exercise some control over family size. Second, in some areas child mortality has declined because of slowly improving nutrition and health care, and so families produce fewer children on the assumption that fewer births are needed to attain a given family size.[23] However, world population will continue to rise even as population growth rates decline, because so many people in the Third World are under the age of fifteen (roughly a third of the population in some countries) and are just reaching the years when they will have children.

Food Production   In recent decades, world food production per person has slowly increased. A major reason was the "Green Revolution" of the 1960s, a major agricultural revolution resulting from new discoveries in plant genetics that enable farmers to greatly increase their production of tropical wheat, rice, and grains (see Chapter 4 for a discussion of genetics). In India, food production grew rapidly after the mid-1960s, and, on the heavily populated island of Java, increased rice production led to a dramatic improvement in the standard of living during the 1970s.[24] One problem with the Green Revolution is that the new crops prosper only in very moist soils, so the Green Revolution cannot occur in dry areas such as the drought-stricken regions of Africa or in areas where irrigation systems cannot be organized. (Scientists are trying to develop seeds that will thrive in dry areas.) Another is that, since the Green Revolution requires some capital investment, it tends to benefit the wealthier rather than the poorer farmers.

The food increase has not been distributed equitably either among countries or within countries, because wealthy people and nations eat far more than do poor people. The result is that many people in the world experience hunger in the midst of improved food production. Some people starve to death today, in the sense that they have nothing to eat. Many more, however, suffer from malnutrition or protein deficiency, which leads to slow death, especially among children. Most of these people live in two poverty belts, one extending across the middle of Africa, where droughts have helped cause famines, and the other beginning around Afghanistan and stretching eastward across South Asia (including Pakistan, India, and Bangladesh). The suffering in these areas is so great that in 1988 Archbishop Renato R. Martino, the Vatican's observer at the United Nations, said: "Hunger has reached such an extent and its victims are so numerous that future generations will undoubtedly regard it as the greatest catastrophe of our times, surpassing in horror and magnitude all the other tragedies that have unfortunately marked the twentieth century."[25]

Sanitation, Housing, Education   Population growth continues to intensify other problems. One is ensuring safe water to urban slum areas and rural peasant villages. Another is housing, especially in large cities, where many families cannot afford the cheapest housing and must live in ramshackle huts or even tents. Another is education, since many children are prevented from attending school because their families need them to earn supplementary income.

Disease   People in poor nations are particularly susceptible to disease. In recent years, diseases such as tuberculosis and cholera have become more common in some areas. Another example is the AIDS epidemic in Africa. Still another is river blindness, an infection that destroys the optic nerve and thus causes blindness. In Burkina Faso (Africa), farmers continue to cultivate rich river lands even though they know river blindness is common there. They assume that they will be blind by middle age, so they feel they must earn money quickly so they will have something to live on after they are blind.[26]

Degradation of the Natural Environment   In the wealthy nations, the basic environmental problems result from overconsumption of resources (food, oil, and so on) and from emission of various waste materials (such as the chemicals that produce acid rain) into the earth's atmosphere. In the Third World nations, the basic environmental problems usually result from poverty, from expanding numbers of people overusing basic resources such as land and water in an attempt to survive. In central Africa, peasants have allowed their cattle to over-graze land along the southern edge of the Sahara Desert, thus destroying the vegetation and gradually turning existing grasslands into desert. In other areas, people needing firewood for cooking and heating have cut down so many trees that whole forests have been destroyed. Still another problem is water scarcity in areas like the Middle East and parts of Africa where the available water is not sufficient for an expanding population.

Some in Third World nations actively try to conserve natural resources. In India, for example, the Chipko Movement of the 1970s and 1980s involved ordinary people who "embraced" trees to prevent lumber companies from chopping them down. Others are more concerned with business and industrial development, saying that they want to emulate the wealthy nations that already have gotten rich through pollution.

Subordination of Women   Women in poor countries confront more problems than do men. As children, they are usually fed less than boys and receive little education. As teenagers, they are often forced into an arranged marriage; some are sold to be prostitutes. As wives and mothers, they work longer hours than their husbands, because they must care for the children as well as provide much of the family's food through gardening. (The husband usually cultivates a cash crop.) If they outlive their husbands, they are often denied any inheritance and sometimes end up as beggars.

In some countries, such as India and China, female infanticide is still practiced because girls are perceived as a drain on the family's resources. In some fundamentalist Muslim countries legal restrictions prevent women from participating in the social, political, and cultural life of their societies.

Some women in some areas have started movements to improve their situation. The Green Belt Movement was founded in Kenya in 1977 by Professor Wangari Maathai, one of the relatively few female professionals in Third World countries. Since then, thousands of Kenyan women have earned income by planting millions of trees that conserve soil and provide firewood. In Chile, "Women for Life" was one of the organizations that campaigned in the 1980s against the brutalities of General Pinochet's military regime and helped bring down that regime in 1990. In India, a Working Women's Forum was founded in 1978 as a union of poor women workers. It set up some health care facilities and also provided small-business loans to poor women. Other examples could be given, but these illustrate some of the grassroots initiatives by women in the Third World. If such initiatives gradually improve the status of women, the results could be dramatic, since birth rates often drop and economic production usually increases when women get access to health care and education.

The condition of women in poor countries was a major focus of a UN Conference on Population and Development held at Cairo in September 1994. At the conclusion of the conference, most of the nations of the world signed a broadly worded document that encouraged them to stabilize world population by providing greater options for women in education and reproductive health care.

Ineffective Governments

Governments of poor nations are often ineffective at dealing with the preceding problems. One common reason is a lack of trained personnel. Another is that government leaders are often so afraid of social unrest—from young people angry about living conditions—that they spend large amounts of money on arms purchases to protect themselves rather than on economic and social projects. A third reason is debt. The increases in oil prices since 1973 devastated many Third World economies. To pay for oil purchases and other needs, many countries borrowed heavily from international lending agencies—such as the World Bank—and from private banks in the First World. By the 1980s, many nations were paying more to the banks in interest and other debt charges than they were receiving in foreign aid, lending some credence to their charges that they were exploited by the rich nations.[27]

Migration   Tens of millions of people migrate each year in search of a better life. Many migrate within a Third World country, from an impoverished rural area to a city. Many others migrate from a poor country to a wealthy nation, such as from Mexico or Haiti to the United States or from an eastern European or north African country to western Europe. This growing movement of peoples constitutes, among other things, a "brain drain," as many of the more talented people leave the Third World countries in which they were born.

THE 1960s AND 1970s: PROPOSALS FOR INTERNATIONAL AID

In the 1960s and 1970s the poor nations created their own organizational structures through which to pressure the rich nations to increase international economic aid programs. The two most important organizations were the nonaligned movement and the Group of 77.

The nonaligned movement was born in 1955 in the Indonesian city of Bandung. The Bandung Conference tried to establish an organization of those states that refused to align themselves with either the American or Soviet alliance systems. As it turned out, no such organization was created, but the "spirit of Bandung"—the spirit of nonalignment—survived.

The Group of 77 developed in 1964 in connection with an international conference known as UNCTAD (*United Nations Conference on Trade and Development*). This conference, held in Geneva, marked the first time that the rich nations of the North negotiated with the poor nations of the South. To pressure the rich nations for greater economic aid, the nations of the South organized themselves into a Group of 77 members (there are now more than a hundred members).

The influence of the nonaligned movement and the Group of 77 peaked in the mid-1970s. The crucial event was the 1973 OPEC oil embargo and the consequent quadrupling of oil prices. The OPEC decisions created a crisis, and both the rich nations and the poor nations called for an international conference to deal with the situation. The two groups of nations differed on what they expected of such a conference.

The result of the demands for a conference was the Sixth Special Session of the UN General Assembly, which began in April 1974. The poor nations were able to push two resolutions through the Special Session. The first was a statement of principle, which called for a *New International Economic Order* (NIEO) based on equality among nations. The second spelled out a program of action to implement the NIEO. It stated that the rich nations should transfer more technology to the Third World and should give Third World nations more control over their own natural resources.

After 1974 the NIEO was the subject of several international conferences. In 1975 a Seventh Special Session of the UN General Assembly was devoted to the issue of Third World economic development. The Paris Conference on International Economic Cooperation, popularly known as the "North-South conference," took place between October 1975 and June 1977, and another North-South conference was held at Cancún, Mexico, in October 1981.

At these conferences, the South pushed for major structural reforms in the international economic order. The reforms desired by the South included: (1) a program to stabilize raw materials (commodities) prices, because fluctuating prices can disrupt the national budgets of poor countries; (2) special aid programs that would concentrate on meeting the basic human needs—food, shelter, and health care—of people in the poorest nations; (3) a "code of conduct" for supranational corporations, which the poor nations believe withhold valuable technology from them while exploiting their mineral and agricultural resources. (Supranational corporations are an explosive issue in many poor countries because of the enormous influence and power the supranationals wield.)

The Europeans responded to Third World demands with a limited economic aid program. The Lomé Convention of 1975 allowed forty-six former European colonies to export products tariff-free to European Community nations and also established a stabilization fund to maintain steady prices for some Third World products.

For the most part, however, NIEO was never implemented. By the 1980s the bargaining power of the poor nations was undermined by regional disparities—some economic success in Asia, economic failure and food crises in sub-Saharan Africa, and debt crises in Latin America. Furthermore, the rich nations opposed NIEO for several reasons. One is that they resisted giving away some of their wealth. Another is that the present world economic structure works to the advantage of the rich nations, because they are the beneficiaries of cheap natural resources and cheap labor from the poor nations. Some scholars now refer to the New International Division of Labor, in which poor nations with low-paid work forces concentrate on producing manufactured products such as automobiles and clothing and the rich nations emphasize advanced-technology areas such as medical research and computer programming.

THE 1980s AND 1990s

Some improvements have occurred in Third World countries since World War II. In 1950 life expectancy in these nations averaged forty years; by 1990 it was sixty-three years. In 1950 twenty-eight of every hundred children in the Third World died before their fifth birthday; by 1990 the number was ten. Instances of many diseases—smallpox, polio, measles—have been greatly reduced. These successes resulted largely from expansion of educational and health services by Third World governments and from international aid.[28] Also, ordinary poor people often help themselves, an example being the Grameen Bank in Bangladesh. The bank was started in 1976 to prove that the poor can profit from and repay loans even though they rarely have collateral. Most loans went for housing construction by the poor and were repaid. By 1990 the bank had grown to over seven hundred branches in more than eighteen thousand villages.[29]

Despite these improvements, the 1980s and early 1990s were not a good time for most Third World countries. Low world commodity prices limited the income of many nations; high world interest rates increased the debt payments of many; and the amount of investments and loans made by the wealthy nations to the poor nations declined. The number of people living in dire poverty changed very little, as rough estimates indicate that at any one time in the 1980s one billion people in the Third World did not have adequate food, water, housing, and health care. The fear is that the number will increase as world population expands.

The chronic poverty afflicting so many people is a major source of the political instability and civil wars in Third World nations. It is also a source of the appeal of "fundamentalisms," doctrinal systems of all types that purport to define absolute truth in an uncertain world. Many Muslims believe in Islamic fundamentalism; a growing number of Hindus are adherents of Hindu fundamentalism; many in North America and an increasing number in Latin America are attracted to evangelical Protestantism; and the belief in free market ideology appears to offer economic salvation to many of the former communist countries in Europe.

While many Third World economies stagnated or declined in the 1980s and 1990s, the wealthy nations often profited from the international economic system. Banking institutions in the wealthy nations got big returns from loans to Third World countries. Consumers in wealthy nations often bought low-priced items made in Third World countries. Arms manufacturers in wealthy nations sold large quantities of weapons to Third World governments. And the formation of trade blocs, such as NAFTA and the European Union, was, among other things, a way for the wealthy nations (the exception being Mexico in NAFTA) to improve their economic status without having to be concerned about Third World poverty.

In the future, however, the wealthy nations will be increasingly involved with Third World countries, for at least four reasons:

1. Transnational problems such as drug smuggling and environmental degradation will require cooperation between rich and poor nations.
2. Population expansion will increase the pressures encouraging people to migrate from poor to rich nations.
3. As the economies of the wealthy nations become more oriented toward high technology, manufactured products will increasingly be made by developing nations and then will be imported by the wealthy nations.
4. After the end of the Cold War, the major sites of political instability and large-scale violence may be in the Third World.[30]

SUGGESTED READINGS

L. S. Stavrianos, *Global Rift: The Third World Comes of Age* (New York: Morrow, 1981), is a comprehensive history of the Third World that is both thorough and factual. Richard Critchfield, *Villages* (Garden City, N.Y.: Doubleday, 1981), is excellent. The first half presents the author's eyewitness descriptions of Third World villages, and the second half offers the author's ideas, many of them very sensible, about how to alleviate Third World problems. A very thoughtful and provocative analysis of the First World–Third World conflict in the 1960s and 1970s is provided by Robert W. Tucker, *The Inequality of Nations* (New York: Basic, 1977). Theodore von Laue, *World Revolution of Westernization* (New York: Oxford Univ. Press, 1987), is a general analysis of the impact of the West on the Third World. Pranay Gupte, *The Crowded Earth: People and the Politics of Population* (New York: Norton, 1984), is a study of the population problem; and Paul Ekins, *A New World Order: Grassroots Movements for Global Change* (London: Routledge, 1992), is an interesting survey of grassroots movements for social and economic change in the Third World.

There are a number of good books on recent Chinese history, but some of the best are John King Fairbank, *The United States and China*, 4th ed. (Cambridge, Mass.: Harvard Univ. Press, 1979); Maurice Meisner, *Mao's China: A History of the People's Republic* (New York: Free Press, 1977); Lowell Dittmer, *China's Continuous Revolution: The Postliberation Epoch, 1949–1981* (Berkeley: Univ. of California, 1987); Stephen W. Mosher, *Broken Earth: The Rural Chinese* (New York: Free Press, 1983); and William H. Overholt, *The Rise of China: How Economic Reform Is Creating a New Superpower* (New York: Norton, 1993). Also on East Asia, see Haing Ngor, *Haing Ngor: A Cambodian Odyssey* (New York: Macmillan, 1988), the memoir of a Cambodian who survived the harrowing years of the Pol Pot regime during the 1970s. A good introduction to the Arab-Israeli conflict is Deborah J. Gerner, *One Land, Two Peoples* (Boulder, Colo.: Westview, 1991). For the Islamic world, see John Obert Voll, *Islam: Continuity and Change in the Modern World* (Boulder, Colo.: Westview, 1982); and John L. Esposito, *Islam: The Straight Path* (Oxford: Oxford Univ. Press, 1991). Basil Davidson, *Let Freedom Come: Africa in Modern History* (Boston: Little, Brown, 1978), is especially good on the African movements for national independence and the problems facing the newly independent nations. Other works include: Martin Meredith, *The First Dance of Freedom: Black Africa in the Postwar Period* (New York: Harper & Row, 1984); Mort Rosenblum, *Squandering Eden: Africa at the Edge* (New York: Harcourt, Brace, Jovanovich, 1987); Sanford J. Ungar, *Africa: The People and Politics of an Emerging Continent* (New York: Simon & Schuster, 1985); and Nelson Mandela, *Long Walk to Freedom* (Little, Brown, 1994), the autobiography of the South African leader. Recent works on Latin America include:

John Mason Hart, *Revolutionary Mexico: The Coming and Process of the Revolution* (Berkeley: Univ. of California Press, 1987); Walter LaFeber, *Inevitable Revolutions: The United States in Central America* (New York: Norton, 1983); Robert Wesson and David V. Fleischer, *Brazil in Transition* (Westport, Conn.: Praeger, 1983); and Penny Lernoux, *Cry of the People* (Garden City, N.Y.: Doubleday, 1980), on human rights abuses by Latin American governments.

NOTES

1. Susan George, "One-Third In, Two-Thirds Out," *New Perspectives Quarterly*, Spring, 1993, pp. 53–54.
2. Rupert Emerson, *From Empire to Nation: The Rise to Self-Assertion of Asian and African Peoples* (Cambridge, Mass.: Harvard Univ. Press, 1962), pp. 17–18.
3. Robert W. Tucker, *The Inequality of Nations* (New York: Basic, 1977), pp. 36–37.
4. John King Fairbank, *The United States and China*, 4th ed. (Cambridge, Mass.: Harvard Univ. Press, 1979), p. 374. The most accurate estimates of the number of people killed between 1949 and 1952 range from two million (Maurice Meisner, *Mao's China*, New York: Free Press, 1977) to five million (Jacques Guillermaz, *The Chinese Communist Party in Power, 1949–1976*, Boulder, Colo: Westview, 1976).
5. Jean Chesneaux, director, *China: The People's Republic, 1949–1976*, trans. Paul Auster and Lydia Davis (New York: Pantheon, 1979), p. 39.
6. Fairbank, p. 418.
7. Fred Halliday, *The Making of the Second Cold War* (Verso, 1983). p. 164.
8. Vaclav Smil, "How Rich Is China?" *Current History*, September 1993, vol. 92, no. 575, pp. 265, 267.
9. John L. Esposito, "Political Islam: Beyond the Green Menace," *Current History*, January 1994, vol. 93, no. 579, pp. 19–21.
10. Basil Davidson, *Let Freedom Come: Africa in Modern History* (Boston: Little, Brown, 1978), p. 307.
11. Roy Willis, *World Civilizations* (Lexington, Mass.: Heath, 1982), II, 1432.
12. Martin Meredith, *The First Dance of Freedom: Black Africa in the Postwar Era* (New York: Harper & Row, 1984), pp. 350–352.
13. Sanford J. Ungar, *Africa: The People and Politics of an Emerging Continent* (New York: Simon and Schuster, 1985), pp. 445–446.
14. Quoted in David K. Willis, "Fighting Famine," *Annual Editions/World Politics*, 1985/86, p. 146.
15. Charles Vanhecke, "Brazil's Poor Get Poorer," *Manchester Guardian Weekly*, August 3, 1982, p. 14.
16. Abraham F. Lowenthal, "Latin America: Ready for Partnership?" *Foreign Affairs*, vol. 72, no. 1, 1992–1993, p. 85.
17. J. Raloff and J. Silberner, "Saving the Amazon," *Science News*, October 4, 1980, pp. 218–221.
18. Penny Lernoux, *Cry of the People* (Garden City, N.Y.: Doubleday, 1980), p. 174.
19. E. Bradford Burns, *Latin America: A Concise Interpretive History*, 5th ed. (Englewood Cliffs, N.J.: Prentice-Hall, 1990), pp. 189–190.
20. Arnold Toynbee, quoted in L. S. Stavrianos, *Global Rift: The Third World Comes of Age* (New York: Morrow, 1981), p. 33.
21. World Bank, *World Development Report, 1993* (New York: Oxford Univ. Press, 1993), pp. 238–239.

22. Ibid., pp. 288–289.

23. Julian L. Simon, *The Ultimate Resource* (Princeton, N.J.: Princeton Univ. Press, 1981), p. 184.

24. Richard Critchfield, *Villages* (Garden City, N.Y.: Doubleday, 1981), pp. 178, 181.

25. Archbishop Renato R. Martino, quoted in L. S. Stavrianos, *Lifelines from Our Past* (New York: Pantheon, 1989), p. 173.

26. Robert Lacville, "The Scourge of River Blindness," *Manchester Guardian Weekly*, January 6, 1991, p. 19.

27. Stavrianos, *Global Rift*, pp. 472–473.

28. World Bank, p. 1.

29. Paul Ekins, *A New World Order: Grassroots Movements for Global Change* (London: Routledge, 1992), pp. 122–123.

30. Donald M. Snow, *The Shape of the Future: The Post–Cold War World* (Armonk, N.Y.: M. E. Sharpe, 1991), pp. 16–17.

CHAPTER 4

Intellectual and Spiritual Issues in a Technological Age

INTRODUCTION

This chapter is about some of the most significant ideas and beliefs in contemporary Europe and North America. To many people ideas and beliefs seem inconsequential when compared with the threat of nuclear war or people starving in the Third World. But ideas and beliefs are extremely important. People want to know in order to understand the world—the world of God, the world of nature, the world of humanity. Thought is a fundamental characteristic of humans.[1] Also, ideas can have practical consequences. Economic theories like socialism and capitalism can determine how and how well people live. Racial ideas like Hitler's have resulted in the deaths of millions of people. When ideas are held by important leaders or by large groups of people, they can become very powerful and sometimes very dangerous forces.

Three important issues debated in the West since 1945 are:

1. The impact of science and technology: What effect have science and technology had on contemporary societies, and what effect are they likely to have in the future?
2. Political theories: How and to what purpose should contemporary societies be governed?
3. The search for meaning: In a technological age, what beliefs, ideas, and values can humans find to give meaning to their lives?

134

SCIENCE AND TECHNOLOGY

Science and technology dominate the contemporary age. Technology in the form of nuclear weapons made the Cold War dangerous. Technology enables Western societies to be affluent. Technology in the form of medical care fuels the population explosion in the Third World, and technology in the form of the Green Revolution increased food production.

Studying modern science and technology is not just a matter of examining scientific discoveries and technological inventions. We must also understand an attitude toward science—knowledge of the natural world—that has deep roots in Western civilization. This attitude is a desire to use science as a means of mastering and controlling nature. Some historians refer to this attitude as the "Faustian ethic," after a Doctor Faust who lived in sixteenth-century Germany and practiced black magic.[2] In popular legend and in many Western literary works, Doctor Faust was portrayed as having sold his soul to the devil in exchange for knowledge and power. The attitude exemplified by the Faustian ethic can be found in the biblical story of the Garden of Eden and in the Greek myths about Prometheus. Adam and Eve ate from the Tree of Knowledge and were expelled from Paradise because they had defied God's instructions. Prometheus stole fire (a symbol of knowledge) from the gods, gave it to man, and was punished by being chained to a rock where each day an eagle came to devour his liver. In these stories, humans desire and gain knowledge, and therefore power, despite the opposition of divine forces. Both stories depict the gaining of knowledge as a dangerous act which can have both good and evil consequences.[3]

One result of the Faustian ethic is what historians label the "Industrial Revolution." Actually, the Industrial Revolution is a series of three distinct revolutions. The First Industrial Revolution began in Europe in the late eighteenth century and produced, among other things, the steam engine, the railroad, and the cotton mill. The Second Industrial Revolution started in the late nineteenth century and resulted in steel, electricity, automobiles, and airplanes.

In the second half of the twentieth century, a Third Industrial Revolution is under way and affects contemporary societies primarily in three areas: (1) the physical sciences, where major developments have occurred in nuclear energy and the exploration of outer space; (2) the biological sciences, where major discoveries have been made in genetics and medicine; (3) the communications and information spheres, where breakthroughs have led to the computer and to telecommunications.

The Physical Sciences

The field of nuclear energy began to develop early in the twentieth century when Albert Einstein formulated his theory of the interchangeability of matter and energy. In 1934 Leo Szilard, a Hungarian scientist, discovered in theory how to produce a nuclear chain reaction. (A chain reaction refers to a neutron's escaping from an atomic nucleus, striking another atom, and splitting it into two lighter atoms. In the process more neutrons are released to strike more atoms. Each splitting, or "fission," of atoms produces energy, so a chain reaction generates a tremendous amount of energy.)

With the outbreak of World War II, research turned to finding military uses for nuclear energy. The Americans and the British, afraid that Nazi Germany would invent an atomic bomb first, quickly established the Manhattan Project, a secret research program designed to produce an atomic bomb. On December 2, 1942, a team of scientists led by an Italian emigré named Enrico Fermi carried out the first sustained nuclear chain reaction in a laboratory at the University of Chicago. After three years of further research and development, the first atomic bomb was tested at Los Alamos, New Mexico, in the summer of 1945. A few weeks later, bombs were dropped on Hiroshima and Nagasaki, and World War II ended.[4]

Since 1945 nuclear energy has been used for making atomic and hydrogen bombs. It has also been used for producing electricity for peaceful purposes, but by the 1970s and 1980s there was growing public resistance in some countries to construction of more nuclear power plants. In addition to fear of a nuclear explosion like the one at Chernobyl, two major problems were of concern. One involved disposal of the highly radioactive wastes produced by nuclear plants; in the mid-1990s no permanent solution for this problem was known. The other involved disposal of the plants themselves. After thirty to fifty years (no one knows exactly how long), the harsh radiation environment in a nuclear plant causes components and systems to wear out. At that point, the plant is so radioactive as to be unusable, and some of the first plants built in the 1950s may be reaching this point in the 1990s. The obvious question is: What does one do with a large radioactive structure that is no longer useful?

Seven scientists look over a Roentgenometer at an atomic-bomb test site at Alamagordo, New Mexico, September 10, 1945. Dr. J. Robert Oppenheimer of the University of California, director of the Los Alamos atomic bomb project, is third from left.

SOURCE: AP/WIDE WORLD PHOTOS.

Nuclear physics also laid the groundwork for development of laser technology. The word *laser* is an acronym for "*l*ight *a*mplification by *s*timulated *e*mission of *r*adiation." A laser is intense, concentrated light that shines at a single wavelength. The light comes from radiation energy released from an atom or molecule.[5] The basic principle of the laser was described by Einstein in 1916, but the first working laser was developed in 1960 by an American engineer, Theodore Maiman. Lasers have been used to conduct delicate eye surgery, to cut and weld steel, to transmit digital information and telephone conversations, and, more frivolously, to produce laser light shows at rock concerts. Other possible uses include the development of laser-carrying robots working in factories and space-based laser weapons. Some scientists believe that lasers will be the technology of the future.[6]

The exploration of outer space began in 1903 at Kitty Hawk, North Carolina, when Orville and Wilbur Wright made the first flight by a powered aircraft, a flight that went a distance of forty yards. Only a little more than fifty years later, in 1957, the Space

Age began when the Soviet Union used massive rocket engines to launch *Sputnik I*, the first artificial earth satellite. In 1961 the Soviet Yuri Gagarin became the first man to fly into outer space and orbit the earth. By the 1960s the Soviets and Americans were engaged in two space "races": one to send men to the moon, which the Americans did in 1969, and the other to use space for military purposes such as spy satellites. (Spy satellites actually served peaceful purposes, because they allowed each superpower to monitor the armaments of the other and thus provided a means of verifying arms control agreements.) By the 1970s space stations and communications satellites were in orbit, the Western Europeans were able to launch their own satellites, and the United States sent unmanned space vehicles to gather data on Venus, Jupiter, and Saturn.[7]

Exploring outer space can be dangerous. In 1986 the American space shuttle *Challenger* exploded, killing seven crew members, including Christa McAuliffe, the first private citizen passenger on a space flight. Also, the superpowers tried to develop space-based weapons. In an attempt to curb superpower competition in space, the United Nations Outer Space Treaty of 1967 prohibited national claims on celestial bodies and the orbiting of weapons of mass destruction. It also established open access to space for all nonaggressive purposes.[8]

The Biological Sciences

In the biological sciences, revolutionary developments have occurred in genetics. During the last third of the nineteenth century, Gregor Mendel discovered the basic principles of heredity. Mendel found that animal and plant characteristics like height and color are carried from parent to offspring in definite, predictable combinations. The units of inheritance which transmit the characteristics are called *genes*.

By the early twentieth century, scientists learned that genes are located in the living cell on long, microscopic bodies called chromosomes, but they did not understand how the genes operated. By the early 1950s the scientists knew that chromosomes are composed primarily of deoxyribonucleic acid (DNA) and that it is the DNA which carries the genetic information. In 1953 an American, James D. Watson, and a Briton, Francis H. C. Crick, working together at Cambridge University, proposed their formulation of the structure of DNA. They demonstrated that DNA is a double-stranded, spiral-shaped molecule that can duplicate itself.[9]

For their discovery Watson and Crick received a Nobel Prize in 1962. But their discovery was only one of many breakthroughs in genetics. By the mid-1960s scientists began to understand the regulatory system by which DNA controls the production of new cells and knew more about how the genetic code works.[10] Recombinant DNA research developed during the 1970s. This is the process, used in medical research, of removing genes from one organism and inserting them into another. By the early 1990s the United States and twenty-five other nations had launched the Human Genome Initiative, an ambitious research project designed to discover all the genetic information in human DNA. (*Genome* is a collective word for all human DNA.)

The new knowledge in genetics not only enabled scientists to start understanding how life begins but also had many practical results. New drugs and chemicals were produced. The Green Revolution, discussed in Chapter 3, resulted from advances in plant genetics. Progress was made toward preventing or correcting human diseases caused by genetic disorders, like sickle-cell anemia and Down's syndrome.

The revolution in genetics has given the human race an awesome power. One example of that power was the growth of cloning, or reproduction of embryos in a laboratory. Cloning of vegetable and animal embryos was done in the 1970s and 1980s; the first human clone was created in July 1993 by Robert Stillman and Jerry Hall of George Washington University. Cloning is likely to raise major religious and moral issues in the future, since many people perceive cloning of human embryos as human arrogance, a human assumption of the power of divine creation. Another example of genetic power is the belief that genetic knowledge can explain, predict, and even modify human behavior. Some highly publicized studies in the 1990s allegedly showed that genes could predispose certain people to crime or to homosexuality, the implication being that a genetic "correction" might be able to eliminate the "aberrant" behavior. It should be noted that the publicity surrounding these studies was often misleading and that few scientists believe there is an absolute correlation between genes and human behavior. (Environment also affects behavior.) A third example of genetic power is the possibility of discrimination against those who show a genetic tendency toward some disease. In the 1970s some U.S. insurance companies denied coverage to some African Americans who had a genetic predisposition for sickle-cell anemia.[11]

Just as significant as the new knowledge in genetics were the advances in medicine. Penicillin and other antibiotics have helped control many infectious diseases. New vaccines have helped prevent measles, smallpox, and polio and enabled many people to live longer and healthier lives (the polio vaccine, developed in the 1950s by Jonas Salk and Albert Sabin, prevented a crippling disease that had primarily afflicted children). By the 1960s and 1970s kidney transplants were being carried out, an artificial heart was created and used with some success, and test-tube babies were being born.

Modern medicine has been of great benefit to humankind. But because many of the advances in medical technology are so expensive that only a relatively few people can afford them, the new technology raises complex moral questions. Who should have access to the marvels of modern medicine? If everyone has access, who will pay the bills for those who cannot afford the enormous costs of debilitating, life-threatening diseases like AIDS? Which diseases ought to receive the most money for research and treatment?

Today more people are living longer, but modern societies have not confronted the question of how people can best benefit from an increased life span. Will older, retired people live out their last years in boredom and gradual physical deterioration, or can modern societies implement new ways for older people to live creative and useful lives?[12]

The Computer and Telecommunications

Science and technology are transforming the way people collect and use information and communicate with each other. Of all the technological marvels of the twentieth century, the computer could become the most significant. Basically, the computer is a device for handling or processing information, so in a sense humans have been using computing devices for centuries (the abacus, for example). In the seventeenth century the first mechanical calculator was developed, and in the eighteenth century an Englishman named Charles Babbage invented a rudimentary computer.[13]

By the 1930s relatively simple computers had been developed independently in Germany, the United States, and Great Britain. The British used their computers to break German military codes during World War II.[14] The first real electronic computer was produced in 1946 by Drs. John Mauchly and J. P. Eckert of the University of Pennsylvania. This machine, named ENIAC (*E*lectronic *Nu*merical *I*ntegrator *a*nd *C*alculator), filled an entire basement and worked only in short bursts because its vacuum tubes kept burning out. Nevertheless, it could work in two hours a problem which would previously have taken a hundred engineers one year to solve.[15]

If computers had remained giant machines like ENIAC, their social impact would be limited because they would be too cumbersome and unreliable to be used for anything other than highly specialized tasks. What changed everything was the invention of the "transistor," a slice of material so small that computers could be miniaturized. The early transistors were wired into computers, but gradually engineers realized that the wiring could be printed on a surface.

By the early 1970s hundreds of thousands of electronic circuits were being printed on a silicon chip the size of a child's fingernail.[16] As a result the microprocessor, the device that does the calculations and logic for the microcomputer, was developed in the 1970s. The new microcomputers are small machines that are inexpensive and can be programmed to perform a wide variety of tasks. By the early 1980s computers were being used to handle routine paperwork, to manage business inventories, to track down criminals, to guide humans into outer space, and to direct communications satellites. By the 1990s a phenomenon called the "information superhighway" referred to a worldwide interconnection among millions of computers and telephones. Through the phones, computer users of all types could share information with others around the globe. Also, computers in the form of robots with artificial intelligence were beginning to perform many routine jobs in factories.[17] Artificial intelligence (AI) was a major area of research in the 1980s and early 1990s, as some computer scientists believed that computer systems could be made to replicate the intelligence of a human brain.

No one knows what the ultimate impact of the computer will be. Computers could create massive unemployment by taking people's jobs and they could endanger people's privacy by collecting and storing personal information. The computer revolution could produce a two-class society with those who understand computers controlling those who lack computer knowledge.[18] But computers could foster economic growth in many industries and free humans from much tedious and dangerous labor. Perhaps the most optimistic prediction is that the computer revolution could gradually lead to a world in which humans would have both more affluence and more leisure time.[19]

While the social impact of the computer is just beginning to affect us, the impact of telecommunications—television, radio— has been growing for several decades. The first experimental televisions were developed in the 1930s, and by the 1970s television had spread to most of the countries of the world. Communications satellites transmitted news and other live broadcasts from all over the world. Television became a dominant form of leisure activity in the Western nations, and some people feared that it was weakening educational achievement by encouraging young people to watch TV programs rather than read and study. Television also affects politics. It can rapidly and graphically publicize important political and social issues, but it usually examines these issues less thoroughly than do newspapers and newsmagazines. It can also, unintentionally perhaps, favor appearance over substance by encouraging those political figures who are photogenic but not especially thoughtful. (One wonders if the awkward, plain-looking Abraham Lincoln could be elected president of the United States in a television age.)

Television influenced many recent political events, examples being the 1989 revolutions in Eastern Europe and the 1989 Tiananmen Square rebellion in China. Many Eastern Europeans were able to access television programs from West Germany before 1989, and those programs revealed the disparity in living standards between Western and Eastern Europe. In effect, television encouraged the Eastern Europeans to rebel against communism. In China, the Tiananmen Square events were televised to the world, thereby embarrassing the Chinese government and making it more difficult for the government to control the rebellion.

The Impact of Science and Technology

The following five topics indicate briefly some of the ways, both positive and negative, in which science and technology are changing the contemporary world.

1. Standard of living: As discussed in Chapter 2, many nations, particularly in Europe and North America, have attained a level of affluence unparalleled in human history. As noted in Chapter 3, even some of the poorer nations have achieved significant gains in standard of living.
2. Weapons technology: Much technological creativity is devoted to developing highly destructive weapons. The nuclear arms race and the continuing acquisition of sophisticated weaponry by many Third World nations (see Chapter 1) threaten to increase the amount of violence in the world.
3. Globalization of information: Communications technologies such as television spread information all over the world, with both positive and negative results.

4. A new conception of humanity: Many writers and scholars are increasingly thinking of the computer as a metaphor for the human brain. For example, some psychologists speak of the input and output (computer terms) of the brain, and some linguists treat language as if it were a programming code (similar to a computer code). Thus, a new conception of humanity may be emerging, one which regards humans as vastly complicated machines or sophisticated computers.[20]

5. The natural environment: Since 1900 world industrial production has increased by a factor of fifty, consumption of fossil fuels has grown by a factor of thirty, and human population has more than tripled.[21] The massive growth of industrialization has produced major changes in the natural environment (see Chapter 2), some of which threaten human well-being and possibly even the very existence of life on our planet. If degradation of the environment continues to increase, the result will be fundamental changes in the ways people live. If, on the other hand, traditional forms of industrialization are fundamentally altered so as to protect the environment, that too would produce fundamental changes in the ways people live.

POLITICAL AND SOCIAL THOUGHT

Political and social thought should always be analyzed with great care, for they can have enormous impact on people's lives. One need only think of the millions who died in Europe because of Nazi racial ideas, the millions who died in Stalin's Soviet Union because of communist political theories, or the African Americans who have been oppressed because of racial ideas. As Sir Isaiah Berlin comments in *Four Essays on Liberty:*

> There has, perhaps, been no time in human history when so large a number of human beings, both in the East and West, have had their notions, and indeed their lives, so deeply altered, and in some cases violently upset, by fanatically held social and political doctrines. . . . When ideas are neglected by those who ought to attend to them . . . they sometimes acquire an unchecked momentum and an irresistible power over multitudes of men that may grow too violent to be affected by rational criticism.[22]

Analyses of Totalitarianism

A major concern of debate has been totalitarianism, a political phenomenon unique to the twentieth century. Despotic regimes have existed throughout the course of history, but before the twentieth century it was not possible to control every aspect of a society. Totalitarianism uses modern communication and organizational techniques to establish total control of the political, social, economic, and spiritual life of a society. During the 1930s and 1940s in fascist Italy, Nazi Germany, and Stalinist Soviet Union, individual freedom was abolished, and all people and groups were integrated into a compulsory political system. Those perceived as political enemies by the rulers were sent to concentration camps or killed.[23] With the destruction of Nazism in World War II and the collapse of communism in the Soviet Union in the late 1980s, totalitarianism largely disappeared from Europe. However, the totalitarian system still survives in some countries, such as China, and it could be revived elsewhere. Moreover, in the 1980s and 1990s some scholars known as postmodernists argued that some forms of thought are totalitarian, in that they impose a particular conception of truth on people (see below).

Totalitarianism threatens anyone who desires a free society. A number of writers have sought to understand why and how a society becomes totalitarian and to show the horror of life in a totalitarian regime. The most prominent of these writers was George Orwell, whose *Nineteen Eighty-Four* (1948) has become one of the most widely cited political novels of our time. Among other things, it helped inspire the dissident movement in the Soviet Union.[24]

Nineteen Eighty-Four is about the state of Oceania, a totalitarian society where everyone wears uniforms, telescreens enable the state to monitor its citizens, and "thought" and "love" are considered crimes. Oceania is controlled by "the Party," and the head of state is "Big Brother." Big Brother's portrait and slogan ("Big Brother Is Watching You") are displayed everywhere. Big Brother and the Party justify their rule by claiming that the other two superstates on earth are plotting war against Oceania.

The protagonist of *Nineteen Eighty-Four* is Winston Smith, whose occupation is to rewrite history. He works at the Ministry of Truth, where language and history are manipulated to reflect the Party's wishes. (Some Party slogans are WAR IS PEACE—FREEDOM IS SLAVERY—IGNORANCE IS STRENGTH.) When meanings of words become confused, rational, independent thought is impossible, and a government can better control its citizens.

Winston begins to rebel against the Party and falls in love with Julia, but both are arrested, tortured, and brainwashed. Winston's torturer is O'Brien, a Party functionary, who explains the essence of the totalitarian state:

> There will be no loyalty, except toward the Party. There will be no love, except the love of Big Brother. There will be no laughter, except the laugh of triumph over a defeated enemy. There will be no art, no literature, no science. . . . There will be no curiosity, no enjoyment of the process of life. . . . But always . . . there will be the thrill of victory, the sensation of trampling on an enemy who is helpless. If you want a picture of the future, imagine a boot stamping on a human face—forever.[25]

For Orwell, *Nineteen Eighty-Four* was not so much a clever satire of Stalinism and Nazism as a warning about the future. He believed that a tendency toward totalitarianism was very strong in the post–World War II world and that any society, including the democratic states, could succumb to it just as easily as Germany and the former Soviet Union had. (According to one writer, the novel gives us our most authentic picture of "a state turned by men themselves into hell.")[26] This tendency toward totalitarianism derived from constant preparation for war, which can lead even a democratic society to accept dictatorship, and from political propaganda, which distorts history and the meaning of words and makes clear political thought impossible.[27]

Another literary figure who used his art to dissect totalitarianism is Aleksandr Solzhenitsyn, a Russian writer who spent eight years in a Stalinist labor camp. When he was released in the mid-1950s, he began to publish novels critical of the Soviet regime.

One Day in the Life of Ivan Denisovich (1962) is the fictional story of Ivan Denisovich Shukhov, an ordinary man who has received a long sentence to a labor camp. We learn about one day in the camp, from reveille to lights out, and what it takes to survive. Shukhov and the other inmates are constantly harassed by the guards. Wearing flimsy prison uniforms, they must work in temperatures well below freezing. For meals they have lukewarm gruel with bits of rotten fish and cabbage leaves. Yet Shukhov continues to feel hope. At the end of this day, he thinks:

> He'd had a lot of luck today. . . .
> Nothing had spoiled the day and it had been almost happy.
> There were three thousand six hundred and fifty-three days like this in his sentence, from reveille to lights out.

The three extra ones were because of the leap years. . . .[28]

Solzhenitsyn's *The Gulag Archipelago, 1918–1956* (1974) demonstrates that the labor camp system was a microcosm of Soviet society. Just as camp prisoners were watched and controlled every day, so were Soviet citizens outside the camps watched and controlled. Life for everyone, whether inside or outside the camps, was a story of material squalor, corruption, and terror. By exposing the Soviet camp system, Solzhenitsyn reveals the human degradation that characterizes a totalitarian system. His work won him the 1970 Nobel Prize for Literature, but his criticism of the Soviet regime resulted in his being expelled from the Soviet Union in 1974. (He returned in 1994.) Nevertheless, Solzhenitsyn's writings were one of the factors that helped undermine and destroy Soviet communism in the 1980s.

Orwell and Solzhenitsyn criticized political totalitarianism. The postmodernists criticized intellectual totalitarianism. Postmodernism was originally associated with several French intellectuals—Michel Foucault, Jacques Derrida, Jean-Francois Lyotard—who from the 1970s into the 1990s criticized what they called "Modernity" and called themselves "post" modernists. Modernity, the dominant form of thought in Western civilization over the last three centuries, was based on modern science and assumed that there are rational, absolutely universal truths in the universe that can be and are known by humans. The essence of modernity, according to the postmodernists, was to insist that "Truth" (whether religious truth or scientific truth or political truth) is absolute and that all right-thinking people would accept the truth. The postmodernists, in contrast, contended that there is no absolute truth, that reality is fluid and open-ended, and that there is no great theory or idea that can explain everything.[29] Some, though not all, postmodernists went so far as to say that there are no truths of any sort. Consequently, the postmodernists often appeared to be radical relativists. Even so, the postmodernists made at least one telling point: that individuals or groups which claim to know the absolute truth act as totalitarians when they try to impose their beliefs and thoughts on others.

Democratic Thought

Until the 1980s, lack of intellectual freedom restricted political debate in the Soviet Union and the Eastern European nations, so the following discussion concentrates on political ideas developed in the Western European and North American nations. In the 1990s these ideas are spreading to the former communist countries, where growing political discussion is an integral part of the process of building new political systems.

Three political attitudes dominate practical politics in the democratic societies: *liberalism, conservatism,* and *democratic socialism.* In addition to these three, a fourth attitude—*environmentalism*—offers a radical critique of the democratic societies.

Liberalism   Since World War II, *liberalism* has been the dominant political attitude in Western Europe and North America, both in terms of the number of its adherents and also in its influence on practical politics. Liberals believe that people are entitled to certain basic rights—freedom of thought and religion—and should be able to live their lives as they see fit. They are also concerned that all people should be able to exercise their freedom effectively. Unlike the conservatives, they support the welfare state, but they are not socialists, because they are sympathetic to private enterprise and wish to limit governmental influence in the economy.

Liberalism is not to be identified with a particular political party or political leader. It is a broad attitude shared by the great majority of people in Western Europe and North America and increasingly by people in the former communist countries. It has been the driving force behind most of the political and social movements in the democratic countries since World War II, for example, the feminist movement, the civil rights movement in the United States, and the creation of the welfare state.

The most articulate and thoughtful exponent of liberalism is the English historian and philosopher Sir Isaiah Berlin. His *Four Essays on Liberty* (1969) is one of the twentieth century's finest exercises in political thought. In this work Berlin states that "those who have ever valued liberty for its own sake believed that to be free to choose, and not to be chosen for, is an inalienable ingredient in what makes human beings human."[30]

To support and encourage this basic freedom, liberal societies have evolved two types of political freedom, one negative, the other positive. Negative freedom refers to restrictions placed on the state or any other agency to prevent interference with the individual. For example, the American Bill of Rights prohibits governmental interference with people's freedom of religion, freedom of speech, and freedom of assembly. Positive freedom refers to the liberty to help shape the political and social institutions of one's country. Positive freedom is necessary because, if an individual is to be able to control his or her destiny, he or she must be able to help direct government.[31]

According to Berlin, this conception of freedom led to the development of the welfare state. The absolute economic freedom that existed in the nineteenth century allowed freedom only to the economically powerful. The poor, who in the name of economic freedom were prevented from forming labor unions, lived in poverty and were not free at all. To correct this situation, liberal societies developed the welfare state to ensure that everyone has a decent standard of living.

Berlin believes that the liberal must always be ambivalent about government. Government can help create the conditions necessary for freedom, but government can become too powerful and therefore a threat to freedom. The liberal both fears the state as a potential instrument of oppression and admires the state as a promoter of freedom and protector of justice for all people.[32]

The basic ideas Berlin elaborated—the belief in the importance of liberty and the belief that the state should promote freedom and justice—have dominated politics in Western Europe and North America since World War II. Furthermore, the influence of these ideas has spread over much of the rest of the world; for example, liberal ideas helped precipitate the collapse of communism in Europe in the 1980s. Another example is the UN Conference on Human Rights held in Vienna in June 1993. Representatives from most governments around the world discussed the need to guarantee basic human rights for all people in all countries. There was much disagreement about exactly what these rights are, as Europeans and North Americans tended to talk about political rights such as the right to vote while Asians emphasized economic rights such as the right to a decent livelihood.

Liberalism has been criticized by the Right and the Left. The conservatives have criticized liberalism for encouraging too much popular participation in government and for being too favorable toward state intervention in the economy. Democratic socialists have criticized it for not supporting more state intervention and for allowing what they perceive as an unjust capitalist economy to survive.

Conservatism   Contemporary *conservatism* has opposed many of the dominant political and social trends of our age. It defends capitalism and opposes most government intervention in the economy, on the grounds that intervention interferes with economic freedom and leads to a paternalistic or even totalitarian state. It is wary of "mass" government—too much democracy—because it believes that most people have neither the ability nor the interest to govern well. The conservative attitude is strong in the Christian Democratic parties on the European continent, the Conservative party in Great Britain, and the Republican party in the United States.

In the 1980s, conservatism was particularly influential in the United States (the Reagan administration) and Great Britain (the Thatcher government), in part because of growing public opposition to government spending on welfare state programs. Religious conservatives, who among other things opposed abortion and supported the right to public prayer in schools, became a major factor in the American political process. In the early 1990s a very popular conservative book was Francis Fukuyama, *The End of History and the Last Man* (1992); Fukuyama celebrated the collapse of authoritarian regimes in the Soviet Union and elsewhere and argued that democracy was the only viable political ideology left in the world.

A theorist who exemplifies many of the attitudes of contemporary conservatism is the Austrian economist Friedrich A. Hayek. Hayek's *The Road to Serfdom* (1944), a classic statement of economic conservatism, argues that government intervention in the economy leads inevitably to a tyrannical state. Writing in the early 1940s, Hayek contended that Western civilization was slowly abandoning economic freedom in favor of socialism. Socialism held out the promise of greater freedom resulting from more equal distribution of wealth, but what it delivered was regimentation of economic life, and hence tyranny.[33]

Hayek believed that socialistic programs always result in either fascism or communism. The only way to maintain human freedom is to preserve economic freedom and competition. In Hayek's words:

> What our generation has forgotten is that the system of private property is the most important guaranty of freedom. . . . If all the means of production were vested in a single hand, whether it be nominally that of "society" as a whole or that of a dictator, whoever exercises this control has complete power over us.[34]

He conceded that the state could provide a minimum standard of living for everyone, but he would not accept economic or social planning.

Democratic Socialism   According to *democratic socialism*, human freedom can be achieved only if all people are released from the social and economic bondage of poverty. Political democracy is not enough; there must be social and economic democracy as well. The battle cry of the democratic socialists is "equality," which means that whatever a society produces should be shared by all its members.

In the 1950s and 1960s the democratic socialists helped inspire creation of the welfare state because they favored economic and social benefits for the poorer classes. Among the European countries, democratic socialist political parties were strong in West Germany, Great Britain, France, and several of the Scandinavian countries. In the United States, democratic socialism was not as powerful, but one of its most articulate advocates was Michael Harrington, an American.

In *Socialism* (1972) Harrington states that humanity's battle with nature has been won and that there are now enough material goods for everyone, if these goods are distributed equitably. Competition for goods can cease, cooperation and equality can become the natural state for humankind, and compulsory work can disappear.[35] In Harrington's view, socialism provides a dream of a better world, a world where machinery liberates humanity. The question is how to turn this dream into a reality.

Harrington's *Toward a Democratic Left* (1968) attempts to define a practical program for democratic socialism. He argues that private business cannot respond to the most urgent social and economic needs of modern societies, because private business is interested only in what is economically profitable and not in solving social problems.

A new approach to social problems must be developed, an approach based on "a social determination of what is economic."[36] Economic and social planning must be carried out by a democratic political authority rather than by private business, and on the local and regional level, so that many people can participate in the planning process. Popular participation would lead to an economic program designed to eradicate poverty and equalize the distribution of material goods. Such a program would provide decent housing, produce genuine full employment, establish a guaranteed annual income for those unable to work, improve educational quality, and create a humane natural and social environment for everyone.[37]

Democratic socialism lost influence in the 1980s and 1990s, partly because the collapse of communism discredited socialism and also because the shrinkage of trade union membership in Europe and North America reduced the size of one of the traditional supports of democratic socialist ideas. However, democratic socialism could easily revive in the future. In the mid-1990s many people in the former communist countries clearly fear the competitiveness of a totally free market economy and want to retain some sort of socialistic welfare state. Furthermore, representatives of the poor nations often assert socialistic arguments when they seek some degree of economic equity with the rich nations (see Chapter 3.)

Environmentalism   Liberalism, conservatism, and democratic socialism accept industrialism, in the sense that most proponents of all three attitudes believe that an industrial economy produces prosperity and is therefore a desirable phenomenon. In recent decades a new political attitude known as *environmentalism* has evolved, and a number of environmentalist writers have strongly criticized modern industrial economies (because of pollution and heavy resource consumption) and argued that many traditional industrial practices must be either greatly modified or eliminated entirely. The American biologist Barry Commoner is an example of an environmentalist who believes that modern industry and technology must be modified and reformed, while the American novelist and essayist Edward Abbey expresses the attitude that in some respects industrialism should be eliminated.

In *The Closing Circle* and *Making Peace with the Planet,* Commoner writes that the ecological failure of modern societies is not caused by technology but by the way these societies use technology. Particularly since World War II, he points out, modern societies have increased production of products that pollute, for example, synthetic rather than natural fibers in clothing and large, high-powered automobiles rather than small, low-powered ones. (Partly in response to environmentalist criticism, the automobile industry has in recent years decreased the size of many automobiles and developed some less wasteful engines.) The result is an environmental crisis that is "somber evidence of an insidious fraud hidden in the vaunted productivity and wealth of modern, technology-based society."[38] According to Commoner, modern societies do not have to give up technology and prosperity, but they do have to learn to use technology in a manner more compatible with the natural environment.

Abbey is much more radical than Commoner. In essays such as *Desert Solitaire* and novels such as *The Monkey Wrench Gang,* he contends that we should stop trying to dominate all of nature with technology and should re-learn the reality that we are a part of nature. In fact, he argues that many natural areas should be left completely free of human-made technologies, for wilderness is essential to civilized living. In Abbey's words, "Wilderness complements and completes civilization. . . . The chief reason so many people are fleeing the cities at every opportunity to go tramping, canoeing, skiing into the wilds is that wilderness offers a taste of adventure, a chance for the rediscovery of our ancient preagricultural, preindustrial freedom."[39]

Nationalism and Ethnic Loyalties

In the late 1980s and 1990s nationalism and ethnic loyalties became increasingly prominent in much of Europe and parts of North America and strongly influenced a number of political events.

A wave of nationalism resulted from the collapse of the Soviet Union and the breakup of the Soviet bloc. The former Soviet Union split into over a dozen new nation-states, and nationalistic, even antiforeigner sentiments became very strong among many people, particularly in Russia and Ukraine. In the eastern European area, nationalistic emotions helped stimulate the Polish rebellion against Soviet control in the 1980s. Nationalism also helped produce the reunification of Germany and the breakup of Czechoslovakia into the Czech Republic and Slovakia. The most violent nationalism erupted in the former Yugoslavia, where Serbian nationalism helped precipitate the war that continues in the Balkan peninsula.

Ethnic loyalties (that is, loyalties to a group defined by cultural, linguistic, or racial ties) became so strong in some areas that it constituted xenophobia (fear or dislike of strangers or foreigners). Examples include the ethnic hatreds in the former Yugoslavia, the anti-immigration sentiments that developed in parts of the United States and several western European countries in the 1990s, and the separatist movement which hopes to have Quebec secede from Canada. What fueled these ethnic loyalties, among other things, were the fears that result from international population movements which bring foreign refugees to the wealthy nations of North America and western Europe and the increasingly globalized economy which removes much economic power from local or even national control. Ethnic loyalty—loyalty to a group of familiar, like-minded people—provides a safe haven and sense of security in a scary world.

THE SEARCH FOR MEANING

A part of being human is to ask about the meaning of things: "What is the meaning of life?" "What is the meaning of history?" "Is there any purpose in nature?" The answers people find help determine what they value and believe, how they live and behave. In the past some societies have agreed about the meaning of life and the values by which people should live. In the Middle Ages of the Western world, Christianity provided a system of beliefs for most people. No such consensus exists in the West today. As one writer has put it, there is "little of anything at all of profound significance that is widely shared by modern man."[40]

The search for meaning is especially difficult in a nuclear age. The threat of mass destruction, among other things, has led some people to conclude that there is no meaning anywhere, while others find meaning either within history or in some form of religious faith. For still others a belief in human progress provides a sense of purpose. These different perspectives will be examined in the following pages.

A World without Meaning

At the beginning of the twentieth century, many Europeans and Americans believed that the world was a rational, orderly place that humans could and did control. Fifty years later, this belief had been replaced by a more pessimistic attitude. The reasons for such a transformation are numerous.

There are the political events of the century. The twentieth century provides considerable evidence of man's inhumanity and irrationality: world wars, concentration camps, nuclear weapons arsenals. There is a fear that industrial civilization dehumanizes people. The size of most modern organizations—governments, businesses, labor organizations—causes people to feel insignificant. There is the spiritual vacuum in which many modern people live. Large numbers of people no longer have confidence in anything. They have lost faith in God and do not believe that a transcendent realm exists. They have also lost faith that science and human reason can produce an improved existence for humanity.

All these factors have produced what one historian calls the "Age of Anxiety."[41] Much of the philosophy, art, and literature in this "Age of Anxiety" expresses the absurdity of the human condition, an attitude which was prominent in the 1950s and 1960s.

The philosophy of existentialism is based on recognition of absurdity. Existentialism derives from the writings of Søren Kierkegaard, Friedrich Nietzsche, and Feodor Dostoevski in the nineteenth century and, in the twentieth century, of Martin Heidegger and Karl Jaspers. Its most famous exponent in the years after World War II was the French philosopher and literary figure Jean-

Paul Sartre, but for purposes of this discussion the work of French novelist and essayist Albert Camus is particularly revealing.

Camus's novel *The Plague* (1947) is one of the best expressions of the existentialist attitude, especially for the 1990s when the AIDS epidemic reminds us that death can strike unexpectedly. On one level, the novel is about a plague which besieges a city, killing the innocent and defeating all efforts to stop it. On another level, the plague is the disease of war and totalitarianism that infected Europe in the 1930s and 1940s. On a third level, the plague is a symbol of an absurd universe in which innocent humans are victims.[42]

For Camus, the only choice for people of integrity is to fight the plague, as Dr. Rieux does when he remains in the plague-ridden city to help the sick. Dr. Rieux defines himself by fighting against the plague and thereby struggling symbolically against the absurdity of the cosmos. Yet, he has no illusions about winning the fight. Humans cannot escape absurdity. At the end of the novel, Dr. Rieux reflects on "the never ending fight against terror . . . by all who, while unable to be saints but refusing to bow down to pestilences, strive their utmost to be healers." He remembers that "the plague bacillus never dies or disappears for good; that it can be dormant for years . . . and that perhaps the day will come when, for the bane and the enlightening of men, it would rouse up its rats again and send them forth to die in a happy city."[43]

The existentialist concept of the meaninglessness of life can also be found in modern art. A particularly good example is *The Merry-Go-Round*, a 1916 painting by Mark Gertler which shows men and women as robots in uniform driven round and round by the machine of war.[44] American novelist Kurt Vonnegut, Jr., also explores the theme of absurdity. His best-known works—*Player Piano* (1952), *Cat's Cradle* (1963), *Slaughterhouse-Five, or the Children's Crusade* (1969)—portray a world without meaning or purpose, where human irrationality and inhumanity are always evident.

In *Slaughterhouse-Five* Vonnegut tells the story of Billy Pilgrim, an American soldier during World War II who is captured by the Germans and taken to Dresden, where he witnesses the city's destruction by American firebombers. As a result, Billy becomes disoriented and begins to move backward and forward in time. He observes his own birth and death several times, and also the deaths of many others. Each time someone dies, Vonnegut writes "So it goes," the implication being that humans have no choice but to accept the irrationality and absurdity of reality.

The theme of irrationality also occurs in *Player Piano*, which tells the story of a World State controlled by technicians. Since

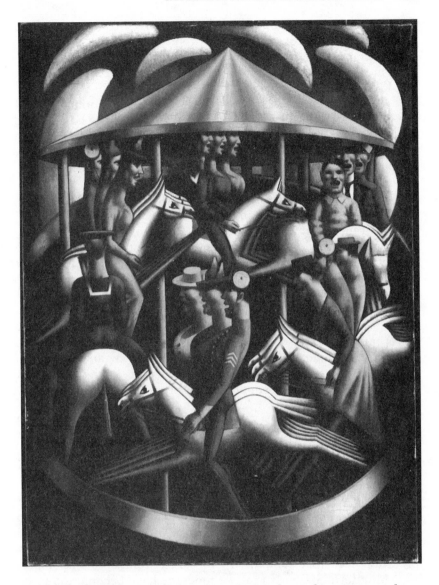

The Merry-Go-Round, a 1916 painting by Mark Gertler, expresses the modern absurdist view of life by depicting people as robots in uniform driven round and round by the machine of war.

SOURCE: The Tate Gallery, London.

most jobs are done by machines, humans have little to do and are bored. The people revolt, but the revolution fails. But before they surrender, the rebels repair the machines they have broken. Vonnegut's message is that, even if the revolution had succeeded, nothing would have changed.[45]

The irrational world described by Camus, Vonnegut, and other twentieth-century artists is a bleak place of little hope. There is no God in the universe, and therefore no meaning or purpose to anything. People are often cruel and inhumane: witness the wars, racism, and concentration camps they continue to inflict on one another.

Yet, despite their belief that the world is irrational and inhumane, the artists of the absurd have found ways for people to live. Camus argued that humans can create their own meanings by affirming their freedom to act. Vonnegut uses humor to laugh in the face of absurdity and portrays love as a healing balm for lonely humanity.

Meaning in History

In recent decades, a number of historians and philosophers have examined the centuries-long historical record in an attempt to find some pattern, some meaning or purpose in the variety of historical events. This form of study is often called the philosophy of history.

William H. McNeill's *The Rise of the West* is a widely influential interpretation of world history. McNeill contends that the twentieth century is a time of technical and institutional creativity during which the first real world community has emerged. Less optimistic are some other writers who perceive the modern period as a time of crisis. Eric Voegelin, for example, argues in *Order and History* that the modern world is dominated by political and moral relativism and that the only remedy is a return to belief in divine spiritual reality. Lewis Mumford in *The Myth of the Machine* offers an interpretation of history sympathetic to the environmentalist perspective. Mumford contends that we moderns have become too fascinated with large-scale machinery and technology and thereby have separated ourselves from the spiritual satisfactions of living in harmony with nature.

David B. King, in *The Crisis of Our Time* (1988), may have delineated one of the major reasons why there is so much debate about the meaning of history and the meaning of life. He says that we are living through a crisis period in the history of Western civilization, similar to a few other crisis periods earlier in Western history. If he is right, the late twentieth century is part of a major turning-point in history, a time of some chaos but also of some creativity.

Christianity

Not everyone believes that the world is absurd. Many people in the twentieth century have found meaning and purpose in religious faith, and their religion helps them define their moral attitudes on such issues as abortion and the gap between the rich and the poor in the world. Examples of religious vitality around the world include the revival of Islamic fundamentalism, the development of liberation theology in Latin America, the growth of evangelicalism in the United States and of Catholicism in sub-Saharan Africa, and the ability of Catholicism to serve as a focus of opposition to the communist regime in Poland.

Within Western civilization, Christianity is the most pervasive form of religion, both because of the number of Christian believers and because of its general cultural influence. Christianity is not as influential as it was five hundred or even two hundred years ago, when the great majority of people in Europe and North America accepted Christian beliefs. In the modern West, religious indifference or nonbelief characterizes a large segment of the population, particularly in Western Europe.

The reasons for the decline in the influence of Christianity are diverse. One is the growing impact of the scientific world view, which demonstrates for many people that there are no supernatural or divine forces in the world. Another is the rise of various secular doctrines—nationalism, socialism, fascism, the belief in progress—which have become substitute religions for many. A third is that churches, particularly in Europe, have often allied themselves with the wealthy, conservative, upper classes and have lost influence with the working class.[46]

But the institutional church has displayed great vigor in recent decades. There has been a rapid growth of evangelical Christianity, especially in the United States but also in Western Europe. Evangelicalism is a form of Protestantism that is theologically conservative. Many evangelicals interpret the Bible literally and do not believe that human reason helps in the search for God.

The beliefs of the evangelicals are not that different from those of traditional Protestants. Like most Protestants, the evangelicals stress the importance of a personal religious experience with God and the centrality of the Bible as the source of God's revelation and authority. What is distinctive about the evangelicals is their ability to communicate to believers the feeling of being "saved." Evangelicalism appeals to many people because it offers emotional comfort and spiritual security. It explains the meaning of life simply and cleanly: God offers eternal salvation in exchange for obedience to God's Word.[47]

Evangelicalism grew dramatically in the United States during the 1970s and 1980s, and evangelical ministers such as Jerry Falwell and Pat Robertson became prominent national figures. One reason for the success of the evangelicals was their ability to use television to create large national audiences for their message. Another was their conservative moral stance—opposition to abortion, the restoration of organized prayer in public schools—at a time when conservatism appealed to many Americans. (The evangelical movement, with its emphasis on conservative moral values and its opposition to secularism, was similar in many ways to the Islamic movement within Muslim societies.)

Another example of revival in the institutional church is the intellectual and spiritual regeneration of Roman Catholicism. The process began with the papacy of John XXIII (1958–1963), who pointed the way to a policy of *aggiornamento*, or "a bringing up to date." Many of John's predecessors had been conservative pessimists who were openly hostile to the dominant political and social trends of the modern world. John was more optimistic about the modern age and wanted the church to reach out to the secular world and to other religions.

As a result of the Second Vatican Council (1962–1965) initiated by Pope John, Catholic intellectuals were granted more freedom of debate on religious matters, Catholic bishops and clergy were given a more active role in the governance of the church, and Catholicism as a whole began a program of increased cooperation with other branches of Christianity and with non-Christian religions. The church began to speak more forcefully about the need to create a more humane world. This posture led to the development of liberation theology in Latin America.[48]

By the 1980s the Catholic hierarchy had become more conservative. Pope John Paul II was less than enthusiastic about liberation theology and was traditionally conservative in his interpretation of many church teachings. But he was a forceful leader who traveled widely to spread the church's message, and he insisted on making the church's voice heard with regard to such modern moral issues as abortion, surrogate motherhood, and homosexuality. He also helped stimulate the 1980s rebellions against communism in Eastern Europe.

Another sign of vigor in Western religion is that a number of prominent theologians have sought to reinterpret Christianity in ways that would be significant to modern people. As a result, the Christian community has experienced a lively theological debate during the twentieth century.

The debate began in response to World War I. Before the war Christian theology had been fundamentally optimistic, teaching that the world was progressing and that the Kingdom of God was being realized on earth. The theology deemphasized human sinfulness and stressed the ability of humans, working in partnership with God, to create a better world.

The war shocked everyone, including a young Swiss theologian named Karl Barth. Barth repudiated the optimistic theology of the nineteenth century in favor of "crisis theology," which recognized that World War I marked a crisis for Western civilization. Crisis theology emphasized the sinfulness of man, clearly apparent from the war, and the radical separation between man and God. For Barth, humans are corrupted by sin and cannot overcome sin or know God through their own efforts. God is the "wholly Other," a transcendent Being completely separated from history. The Kingdom of God cannot be realized on earth. Yet, because God reaches out to people through His self-revelation in Jesus Christ, people can attain salvation by God's grace. Barth's approach, then, is a reaffirmation of traditional Christian themes, and for this reason the Barthian school of thought is often called "neo-orthodoxy." Neo-orthodoxy has been the most influential movement in Protestant theology during the twentieth century.[49]

An interesting Catholic thinker is the Swiss theologian Hans Küng, who is a leader in ecumenical theology. Küng was a theological advisor to the Second Vatican Council, but after the 1960s he became sharply critical of some Catholic doctrines and is no longer recognized by the Church as an official Catholic theologian. Nevertheless, he has written a number of important books, including *On Being a Christian* (1976) and more recently *Global Responsibility: In Search of a New World Ethic* (1991). Küng believes that the world's major religions share a common ethical core, although each is rooted in its own different comprehension of divinity. Küng hopes and believes that shared ethical attitudes will lead to a new world moral order that is ecologically oriented. Specifically, he argues that humans should not use technologies that cause more problems than solutions, that the common good should have priority over individual self-interest as long as human rights are protected, that arms proliferation must be halted, and that the ecosystem must be protected.

A new phenomenon in the 1980s and 1990s is the growth of feminist theology, accompanied by increased visibility of women in religious vocations. For example, German theologian Uta Ranke-Heinemann published *Eunuchs for the Kingdom of Heaven,* in which she sharply criticized the Catholic hierarchy's hostility to women and to sexuality. In North America and Europe, women are increasingly being ordained as ministers in several Protestant denominations, and some branches of Judaism ordained women rabbis. However, conservative Protestant denominations refused to ordain women, and the Catholic hierarchy prevented women from becoming priests.

Theology is only one way in which the Christian message has been presented. Another is the modern novel. One of the most prominent Christian writers of the contemporary era was the German short-story writer and novelist Heinrich Böll. His best-known novels include *The Train Was on Time* (1949), *The Unguarded House* (1954), and *Billiards at Half Past Nine* (1959). In his early works, Böll was primarily concerned with events of the Nazi era and World War II. He revealed the stupidity of war and the spiritual and material degradation that war produces. His later works turn to the mindless hedonism and overindulgent materialism of postwar Germany.

In all his writings, Böll examines his themes with compassion and irony. Ultimately, he was a Christian novelist who sought to apply the values of a traditional faith to the problems of modern people. He wanted to apply the healing power of Christian love to the modern world.[50]

Another Christian writer was the American essayist and novelist Walker Percy. Percy's novels—*The Moviegoer, The Last Gentleman, Love in the Ruins,* and *The Thanatos Syndrome*—explore the spiritual problems of modern people. Percy was relentlessly critical of Western technological civilization. He believed that, despite all the technological marvels, modern people suffer from a spiritual emptiness that is responsible for much of the violence and warfare of the twentieth century.

In *Love in the Ruins,* Percy began: "Now in these dread latter days of old violent beloved U.S.A. and of the Christ-forgetting Christ-haunted death-dealing Western world. . . ." Later in the novel, the protagonist, Dr. Thomas More, reads about World War I and says: "Here began the hemorrhage and death by suicide of the old Western world: white Christian Caucasian Europeans, sentimental music-loving Germans and rational clear minded French-men, slaughtering each other without passion."[51]

In this violent, spiritually empty world, the protagonists of Percy's novels are pilgrims looking for answers to their spiritual questions. In an essay entitled "The Message in the Bottle," Percy compares modern people to castaways on an island who roam the beaches looking for a message in a bottle. The message, Percy suggested, is news from God which must be accepted on faith.[52]

The Doctrine of Progress

Many people, including some who consider themselves Christians, place their ultimate faith in the doctrine of progress. They find meaning and purpose in the pursuit of happiness on this earth. They recognize that the twentieth century has seen many barbarous and inhumane acts. Yet they believe in progress for several reasons. One is the continuing technological advancement that has led to improved living conditions for most people in the Western world. Another is the continued growth of human knowledge, particularly in the natural sciences. A third is the fuller realization of ideals of personal freedom and social equality in Western Europe and North America since World War II.[53]

One of the most articulate and persuasive advocates of the belief in progress was the American philosopher Charles Frankel. In *The Case for Modern Man* (1955) and *The Democratic Prospect* (1962), Frankel argued that human progress was the result of the "revolution of modernity"—material progress, intellectual progress, and "a moral revolution of extraordinary scope, a radical alteration in what the human imagination is prepared to envisage and demand."[54]

Frankel wrote that human expectations are higher because of the progress made in recent centuries. To some degree, these higher expectations have been frustrated by the wars and other evils of the twentieth century, and as a result many people have allowed pessimism to destroy their faith in humanity. Against the pessimists, Frankel contended that the revolution of modernity could and should continue. He conceded, of course, that progress is not inevitable. Yet, he believed that progress had taken place in the past, that more progress was possible in the future, and that humans are always capable of improvement.

The strongest support for the doctrine of progress comes from ordinary people all over the world. The belief in progress has become the faith of the masses. It provides hope for many Third

World peoples and inspires most of the revolutionary movements around the world. In Europe and North America, progress is the official belief of virtually every society.

SUGGESTED READINGS

The best way to study contemporary intellectual history is to read some of the works cited in the text. In addition, there are several good studies which offer broad surveys of intellectual history. Franklin L. Baumer, *Modern European Thought: Continuity and Change in Ideas, 1600–1950* (New York: Macmillan, 1977), and Richard Tarnas, *The Passion of the Western Mind* (New York: Ballantine, 1991) are excellent surveys of modern European thought.

On more specific topics, the following are particularly good. John T. Hardy, *Science, Technology and the Environment* (Philadelphia: Saunders, 1975), presents a clear and intelligent explanation of the major breakthroughs made by modern scientists. Edward McNall Burns, *Ideas in Conflict: The Political Theories of the Contemporary World* (London: Methuen, 1963), is a good introduction to political thought in the contemporary world. For existentialism and the philosophy of the absurd, two good sources are Charles B. Harris, *Contemporary American Novelists of the Absurd* (New Haven, Conn.: College & University Press, 1971), and Jean E. Kennard, *Number and Nightmare: Forms of Fantasy in Contemporary Fiction* (Hamden, Conn.: Archon Books, 1975). An excellent analysis of religious thought is James C. Livingston, *Modern Christian Thought: From the Enlightenment to Vatican II* (New York: Macmillan, 1991). On the doctrine of progress, two very good recent studies are W. Warren Wagar, *Good Tidings: The Belief in Progress from Darwin to Marcuse* (Bloomington: Indiana University Press, 1972), and Robert Nisbet, *History of the Idea of Progress* (New York: Basic, 1980). Finally, an invaluable reference work for intellectual history is the five-volume *Dictionary of the History of Ideas* (New York: Scribner's, 1973).

Recent publications in intellectual history are far too numerous to mention, since thousands of novels, plays, scientific treatises, philosophical and political works are produced every year. A few, however, are especially interesting and representative. See Walter A. McDougall, *The Heavens and the Earth: A Political History of the Space Age* (New York: Basic, 1985), for an excellent analysis of the impact of space exploration on Western societies. François Jacob, *Logic of Life: A History of Heredity* (New York: Pantheon, 1982), is an insightful history of the revolution in genetics; and Ruth Hubbard and Elijah Wald, *Exploding the Gene Myth* (Boston: Beacon, 1993), evaluates many of the controversial issues in contemporary genetics research. J. David Bolter, *Turing's Man: Western Culture in the Computer Age* (Chapel Hill: Univ. of North Carolina Press, 1984), is good on the cultural significance of computers. Hans Küng, *Global Responsibility: In Search of a New World Ethic* (New York: Crossroads, 1991), is a provocative analysis by one of the leading contemporary theologians. Isaiah Berlin, *The Crooked Timber of Humanity* (New York: Vintage, 1992), is an excellent collection of essays by the greatest liberal political thinker of the twentieth century.

NOTES

1. Franklin L. Baumer, *Modern European Thought: Continuity and Change in Ideas, 1600–1950* (New York: Macmillan, 1977), p. 518.
2. David S. Landes, *The Unbound Prometheus: Technological Change and Industrial Development in Western Europe from 1750 to the Present* (Cambridge, Eng.: Cambridge Univ. Press, 1972), p. 24.
3. Ibid., p. 555.
4. John T. Hardy, *Science, Technology and the Environment* (Philadelphia: Saunders, 1975), pp. 161, 163–164.
5. Ibid., p. 85.
6. "The Dazzle of Lasers," *Newsweek*, Jan. 3, 1983, pp. 36, 40.
7. Walter A. McDougall, *The Heavens and the Earth: A Political History of the Space Age* (New York: Basic Books, 1985), pp. 189, 273, 428.
8. Walter A. McDougall, "Technocracy and Statecraft in the Space Age—Toward the History of a Saltation," *American Historical Review*, 4 (October 1982): 1010, 1020–1021.
9. Hardy, pp. 131–132; and Lawrence Lessing, "Into the Core of Life Itself," in James D. Ray, Jr., and Gideon E. Nelson, *What a Piece of Work Is Man* (Boston: Little, Brown, 1971), pp. 24–27.
10. Lessing, p. 24.
11. John Horgan, "Eugenics Revisited," *Scientific American*, June 1993, vol. 268, no. 6, pp. 124, 131.
12. Leon R. Kass, "The Case for Mortality," *The American Scholar* (Spring 1983): 178. This article is an excellent discussion of the spiritual, moral, and political issues raised by increased human life span.
13. Christopher Evans, *The Micro Millennium* (New York: Washington Square Press, 1979), pp. 8, 15.
14. "Big Dimwits and Little Geniuses," *Time*, Jan. 3, 1983, p. 30.
15. Hardy, pp. 61–62.
16. "Big Dimwits and Little Geniuses," pp. 31–32.
17. William J. Cromie, "Robots: A Growing, Maturing Population," *Sci Quest*, 54 (March 1981): 12.
18. Jan Stewart, "Computer Shock: The Inhuman Office of the Future," *Saturday Review*, June 23, 1979, pp. 14, 17.
19. Evans, pp. 174, 256–258.
20. J. David Bolter, *Turing's Man: Western Culture in the Computer Age* (Chapel Hill: Univ. of North Carolina Press, 1984), pp. 11, 42.
21. Jim MacNeill, "Strategies for Sustainable Economic Development," *Scientific American*, 261, no. 3 (September 1989), p. 155.
22. Isaiah Berlin, *Four Essays on Liberty* (London: Oxford Univ. Press, 1969), pp. 118–119.
23. Karl Dietrich Bracher, "Totalitarianism," *Dictionary of the History of Ideas*, ed. Philip P. Wiener (New York: Scribner's, 1973), IV: 406–408.
24. Ludmilla Alexeyeva, *Soviet Dissent: Contemporary Movements for National, Religious, and Human Rights*, trans. by Carol Pearce and John Glad (Wesleyan Univ. Press, 1985), p. 449.

25. George Orwell, *Nineteen Eighty-Four,* in *Orwell's Nineteen Eighty-Four: Text, Sources, Criticism,* ed. Irving Howe (New York: Harcourt, Brace, & World, 1963), p. 118.

26. Bernard Crick, *George Orwell: A Life* (Boston: Little, Brown, 1980), pp. 397–398.

27. Ibid., pp. 395, 398.

28. Aleksandr Solzhenitsyn, *One Day in the Life of Ivan Denisovich,* trans. Max Hayward and Ronald Hingley (New York: Praeger, 1963), pp. 209–210.

29. Richard Tarnas, *The Passion of the Western Mind* (New York: Ballantine, 1991), pp. 395–402.

30. Berlin, p. lx.

31. Ibid., pp. 122–124, 131.

32. Ibid., pp. xlv–xlvi, lxii.

33. Friedrich A. Hayek, *The Road to Serfdom* (Chicago: Univ. of Chicago Press, 1944), p. 34.

34. Ibid., pp. 103–104.

35. Michael Harrington, *Socialism* (New York: Saturday Review Press, 1972), p. 344.

36. Michael Harrington, *Toward a Democratic Left* (Baltimore: Penguin, 1968), pp. 19–23.

37. Ibid., pp. 75–76, 102.

38. Barry Commoner, *The Closing Circle: Nature, Man, and Technology* (New York: Knopf, 1972), p. 295.

39. Edward Abbey, *Down the River* (New York: Plume, 1991), p. 118, 120.

40. Nathan A. Scott, Jr., "The Broken Center: A Definition of the Crisis of Values in Modern Literature," in William V. Spanos, ed., *A Casebook on Existentialism* (New York: Crowell, 1966), p. 166.

41. Franklin L. Baumer, "Age of Anxiety," in Franklin L. Baumer, ed., *Main Currents of Western Thought,* 2nd ed. rev. (New York: Alfred A. Knopf, 1967), pp. 592–593.

42. Bernard C. Murchland, "Albert Camus: The Dark Night before the Coming of Grace?" in Germaine Brée, ed., *Camus: A Collection of Critical Essays* (Englewood Cliffs, N.J.: Prentice-Hall, 1962), p. 62.

43. Albert Camus, *The Plague,* trans. Stuart Gilbert (New York: Random House, 1947), p. 278.

44. Baumer, *Modern European Thought,* pp. 404, 432.

45. Charles B. Harris, *Contemporary American Novelists of the Absurd* (New Haven, Conn.: College & University Press, 1971), pp. 65–66, 69–70.

46. Hugh McLeod, *Religion and the People of Western Europe, 1789–1970* (Oxford, Eng.: Oxford Univ. Press, 1981), pp. 26, 71–72, 98–99.

47. Robert K. Johnston, *Evangelicals at an Impasse: Biblical Authority in Practice* (Atlanta: John Knox, 1979), pp. 3–4; and David O. Moberg, "Fundamentalists and Evangelicals in Society," in David F. Wells, and John D. Woodbridge, eds., *The Evangelicals: What They Believe, Who They Are, Where They Are Changing* (Nashville, Tenn.: Abingdon, 1975), pp. 157, 159.

48. James C. Livingston, *Modern Christian Thought: From the Enlightenment to Vatican II* (New York: Macmillan, 1971), pp. 492, 495, 497.

49. Ibid., pp. 328–329, 341.

50. W. E. Yuill, "Heinrich Böll," in Brian Keith-Smith, ed., *Essays on Contemporary German Literature* (London: Oswald Wolff, 1966), IV: 142–143, 148, 155–156.

51. Walker Percy, quoted in Robert Coles, *Walker Percy: An American Search* (Boston: Little, Brown, 1978), pp. 192, 194.

52. Walker Percy, *The Message in the Bottle* (New York: Farrar, Straus & Giroux, 1975), pp. 143–144.

53. W. Warren Wagar, *Good Tidings: The Belief in Progress from Darwin to Marcuse* (Bloomington: Indiana Univ. Press, 1972), pp. 240–241, 353.

54. Charles Frankel, *The Case for Modern Man* (New York: Harper, 1955), pp. 208–209.

Epilogue

The disintegration of the Soviet Union and the collapse of the communist systems in Europe from 1989 to 1991 mark the end of a historical era, in several respects. They mark the end of an era that began in the mid-1940s, the Cold War struggle between the United States and the Soviet Union. They mark the end of an era that began in 1917 with the Bolshevik Revolution in Russia and was characterized by communist attempts to overthrow capitalism and revolutionize European societies. They mark the end of an era that began around 1890, an era of great power conflicts and large-scale arms races that centered in Europe and led to World War I, World War II, and the Cold War. They mark the end of a revolutionary era in Europe that began in 1789 with the French Revolution, continued with the unsuccessful revolutions of 1848, and concluded with the communist revolutions in Russia and Eastern Europe in the twentieth century.

The end of an era means the end of some familiar certainties (such as the Cold War division of Europe) and the beginning of a new period that is more uncertain. Many of the forces making for uncertainty and instability in the 1990s have been discussed in this book. They include:

1. An increasing assertiveness by ordinary people, manifested in demands for democratization (for example, by blacks in South Africa) and in demands for ethnic independence (for example, by the various ethnic groups in the former Yugoslavia)
2. The growing destructiveness of military violence throughout the world, caused in part by the availability of powerful, sophisticated weaponry
3. The expansion of globalism, manifested in global com-

165

munications and in the global economy of supranational corporations
4. The increasing awareness of environmental problems that will limit to some degree the ways in which human societies pursue economic development
5. The new technologies of the Third Industrial Revolution that transform every society in which they operate

The power which modern technologies put in human hands (examples being weapons technology and medical technology) makes the 1990s a time of both great destructiveness and great creativity. One fundamental question permeates everything today: Will technology be the means by which we destroy ourselves, or will it enable us to create a good life for most people? Human destiny increasingly lies in human hands, in the political and ethical choices by which individuals and societies decide how to use various technologies. For better or worse, we will have growing influence on what happens to us and our planet.

Index